G-6657

C Instruments (Treble Clef)

DEVELOPING MUSICIANSHIP THROUGH IMPROVISATION

Christopher D. Azzara
Richard F. Grunow

1

GIA Publications, Inc.
Chicago

Developing Musicianship through Improvisation – C Instruments (Treble Clef)
Christopher D. Azzara
Richard F. Grunow

G-6657
ISBN-10: 1-57999-535-7
ISBN-13: 978-1-57999-535-5

Layout and music engravings: Paul Burrucker
Copy editor: Elizabeth Bentley
Recorded and mixed by Rob LaVaque in the Gravity Pool

Copyright © 2006 GIA Publications, Inc.
7404 S. Mason Ave., Chicago 60638
www.giamusic.com

Printed in the United States of America

CONTENTS

INTRODUCTION

Do you know someone who can improvise? Chances are he or she knows a lot of tunes and learns new tunes with relative ease. It seems that improvisers can sing and/or play anything that comes to mind. Improvisers interact in the moment to create one-of-a-kind experiences. Many accomplished musicians do not think of themselves as improvisers, yet if they have something unique to say in their performance, they are improvisers. In that sense, we are all improvisers, and it is important to have opportunities throughout our lives to express ourselves creatively through improvisation.

Improvisation in music is the spontaneous expression of meaningful musical ideas—it is analogous to conversation in language. As presented here, key elements of improvisation include personalization, spontaneity, anticipation, prediction, interaction, and being in the moment. Interestingly, we are born improvisers, as evidenced by our behavior in early childhood. This state of mind is clearly demonstrated in children's play. When not encouraged to improvise as a part of our formal music education, the very thought of improvisation invokes fear. If we let go of that fear, we find that we are improvisers. Improvisation enables musicians to express themselves from an internal source and is central to developing musicianship in all aspects of music.

The process of learning music is much the same as the process of learning a language. Think for a moment about how you learned language. First, you listened to language. From birth and even before, you were surrounded by the sound of language and conversation. You absorbed these sounds and became acculturated to the language. Soon you began to imitate the words and phrases you heard spoken by your parents and siblings. Before you were successful at imitating, you were praised for your efforts and encouraged to "babble" even when the sounds you were making did not make complete sense to others. Eventually you began to associate words (names) with people, things,

feelings, desires, etc., and you began to make statements and ask questions that were your own. You began to think and improvise in the language, and your interaction with parents and siblings was crucial to your language acquisition. After several years of developing your ability to think and speak, years of being surrounded by print, and years of being read to by others, you learned to read and write. You learned to read and write with understanding because of the experiences you had listening, thinking, and speaking.

Developing Musicianship through Improvisation offers an approach to learning music that is similar to the process for learning language. And just as it is possible for everyone to learn a language and engage in meaningful conversation, it is also possible for everyone to engage in meaningful improvisation, which is at the core of the music learning process. Like conversation in language, interaction with others is crucial. In this book, you are asked to listen to music and sing and play melodies and bass lines by ear. The objective is *not* to memorize the tunes. After all, you didn't memorize your speech as a child. Rather, the objective is to internalize so many melodies and bass lines that you begin to hear harmonic progressions (the changes, or patterns in music) and generate your own melodic lines.

At the same time you build a repertoire of tunes and a sense of musical style, you develop an understanding of harmonic progression, harmonic rhythm, and the aural skills you need to listen to music meaningfully and to interact expressively with others. Throughout these materials you will build a vocabulary of tonal patterns, melodic phrases, rhythm patterns, and rhythm phrases to apply in many ways. As a part of *Developing Musicianship through Improvisation* you will read and write music, thus connecting your improvisation to meaningful experiences with notation. The objective is to read and write music with comprehension. You will hear and understand the music documented on the page in the context of what you have created and improvised. You will also gain a greater understanding of music you hear in everyday experiences.

When reading music, it is important to remember that notation is the documentation of a creative process. Learning to read and write music should be presented in light of that creativity. Developing your musicianship through improvisation provides a context for reading and composing music with comprehension. When musicians express themselves by putting together their own musical thoughts in composition, they can create, develop, and reflect on musical ideas. Composers are able to "go back" or "move forward" in time as they create. This reflection and revision process is a good way to discover relationships in music, and, as a result, to improve your overall musicianship. There is a powerful relationship among listening, improvising, reading, writing, and analyzing music. Each has the potential to influence the other in significant ways when presented in the context of improvisation.

With the goal of improving your musicianship, each unit in *Developing Musicianship through Improvisation* is based on a familiar tune. Each unit contains six parts: 1) Repertoire; 2) Patterns and Progressions; 3) Improvising Melodic Phrases; 4) Learning to Improvise – Seven Skills; 5) Reading and Writing; and 6) Learning Solos.

Improving your musicianship will promote more spontaneous and meaningful music-making. Regardless of your musical background, it is never too late to begin learning tunes and harmonies by ear. This process is at the heart of improvisation, and it is perhaps the most exciting aspect of *Developing Musicianship through Improvisation.*

DEVELOPING MEANINGFUL IMPROVISATIONS

The following are additional suggestions for your continued growth as an improviser. The suggestions and the improvisation rating scale that follow provide you with many ways to improve your musicianship as you acquire the skills presented in *Developing Musicianship through Improvisation.* To get started, you may wish to practice one or two of the following concepts at a time. With experience, you will internalize these ideas and develop more meaningful improvisations.

A good place to start this process is listening to other musicians. Become aware of how improvisers:

- personalize melodies with expressive phrasing, dynamics, and tonal and rhythmic variation.
- are spontaneous and in the moment.
- play with space (silence).
- interact with each other.
- develop motives.

- understand harmony and rhythm by ear.
- can play anything that comes to mind.

Developing Musicianship through Improvisation will help you to develop the principles listed above and will also assist you with the following ideas for improving your skills as an improvising musician.

- Learn a repertoire of tunes and improvised solos *by ear* from other musicians and by listening to recordings. Building a large repertoire of tunes by ear will provide a basis for developing improvised solos.
- Listen to improvised music like an improviser— notice the spontaneous interaction.
- Learn harmony by ear.
- Learn a harmonic, rhythmic, and expressive vocabulary by ear.
- Take risks—try out some new ideas.
- Surround yourself with others working on the same principles.

v

ASSESSING YOUR LEARNING

Consider the following rating scale as a means of assessment and feedback
for improving improvisation skills.

Improvisation Rating Scale

Improvisation (Additive Dimension, 0–5)

Try to include all of the following criteria in your improvisations. Circle all that apply. The improviser:

1   performs a variety of related ideas and reuses material in the context of the overall form (thus the performance contains elements of unity and variety).
1   demonstrates motivic development through tonal and rhythm sequences.
1   demonstrates effective use of silence.
1   demonstrates an understanding of tension and release through resolution of notes in the context of the harmonic progression.
1   embellishes notes and performs variations of themes.

Rhythm (Continuous Dimension, 0–5)

Try to establish a cohesive solo rhythmically—develop rhythmic motives in the context of the overall form. As solos improve, indicate progress by circling one of the following. The improviser:

1   performs individual beats without a sense of the meter.
2   demonstrates a rhythmic feeling of the meter throughout.
3   employs various contrasting rhythm patterns without a sense of rhythmic motivic development.
4   begins to develop and relate rhythmic ideas in some phrases.
5   establishes a cohesive solo rhythmically—develops rhythmic motives in the context of the overall form.

Expressive (Additive Dimension, 0–5)

Try to include all of the following criteria in your improvisations. Circle all that apply. The improviser:

1   demonstrates a sense of musical interaction (e.g., melodic dialogue alone, or musical conversation among performers).
1   demonstrates an understanding of dynamics.
1   demonstrates an understanding of musical style and characteristic tone quality.
1   demonstrates a sense of appropriate articulation.
1   demonstrates an understanding of appropriate phrasing.

Harmonic Progression (Continuous Dimension, 0–5, Major/Minor–Tonic and Dominant)

This dimension will vary depending upon the harmonic vocabulary of the tune. Try to perform all patterns in all functions correctly. As solos improve, indicate progress by circling one of the following. The improviser:

1   performs first and/or last note correctly.
2   performs some patterns in one function correctly (tonic reference).
3   performs all patterns in one function correctly (tonic reference).
4   performs all patterns in one function (tonic) correctly and some patterns in one other function correctly.
5   performs all patterns in tonic and dominant functions correctly.

Harmonic Progression (Continuous Dimension, 0–5, Major/Minor–Tonic, Subdominant, and Dominant)

This dimension will vary depending upon the harmonic vocabulary of the tune. Try to perform all patterns in all functions correctly. As solos improve, indicate progress by circling one of the following. The improviser:

1   performs first and/or last note correctly.
2   performs all patterns in one function correctly (tonic reference).
3   performs all patterns in one function (tonic) correctly and some patterns in one other function correctly.
4   performs all patterns in two functions correctly.
5   performs all tonic, dominant, and subdominant patterns (functions) correctly.

RHYTHM SYLLABLES AND SOLFÈGE

While you are building a repertoire of songs and a sense of musical style and harmonic progression, you will also be building a vocabulary of solfège (tonal syllables), rhythm syllables, and names for the tonalities, meters, and functions in the melodies you are singing and playing. Syllables help you to organize musical thoughts so that you can increase your comprehension and make musical inferences. The names of the meters, tonalities, and functions provide a means for you to organize music by ear—a kind of aural classification system. For example, in duple and triple meters you learn large beat (macrobeat) and small beat (microbeat) rhythm functions; in major and minor tonalities you learn tonic and dominant harmonic functions. These tools help you group notes into patterns, patterns into phrases, and phrases into the overall form of the music. In this context, you will begin to improvise more meaningfully. Solfège and rhythm syllables are also useful tools in making the connection from the ear to notation—the symbols of music—both when reading and composing.

The rhythm syllables in this book and on the accompanying CD are based on the rhythm syllables used in *Jump Right In: The Instrumental Series*.[1] Remember, when learning syllables, always perform them. Sing the solfège and chant the rhythm syllables rather than say them.

RHYTHM SYLLABLES

Unit 1 – "Long, Long Ago"
Meter: Duple
Syllables: ♩ = DU; ♫ = DU DE

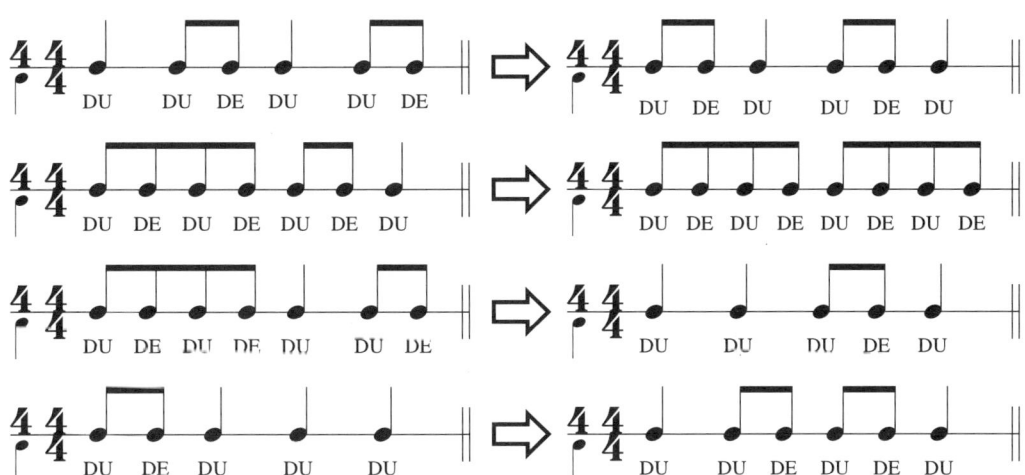

---

1. For more information on the classification names, rhythm syllables, and solfège, please refer to the Teacher's Guide for *Jump Right In: The Instrumental Series* for winds, percussion (Grunow, Gordon, and Azzara, GIA Publications, Inc., 1999, 2001) and strings (Grunow, Gordon, Azzara, and Martin, GIA Publications, Inc., 2002).

Unit 2 – "Mary Ann"

Meter: Duple (Latin Style)

Syllables: ♩ = DU; ♫ = DU DE; ♬ = DU TA DE TA

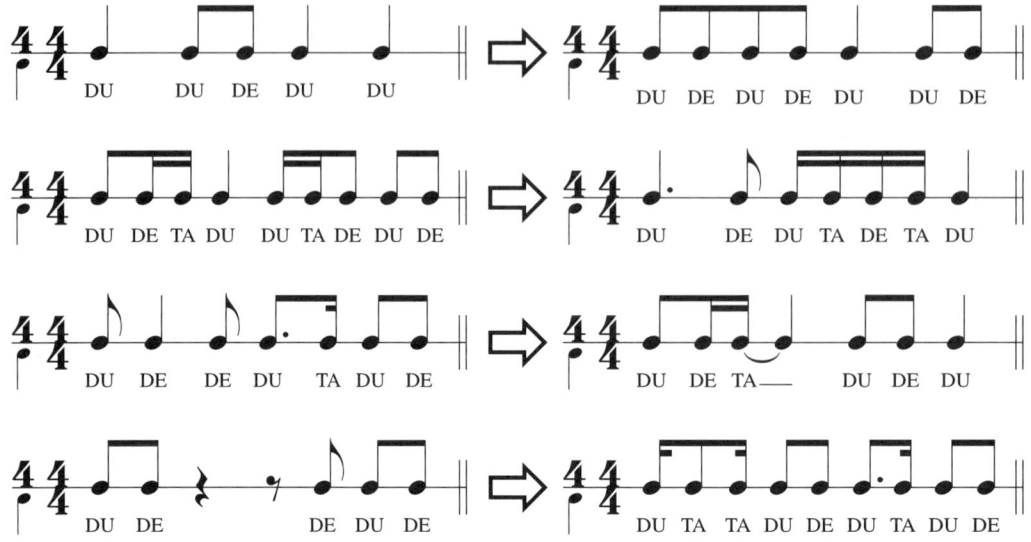

Unit 3 – "Joshua"

Meter: Duple (Swing Style)

Syllables: ♩ = DU; ♩♩ = DU DE; ♬ (swing) = DU DI DE DI

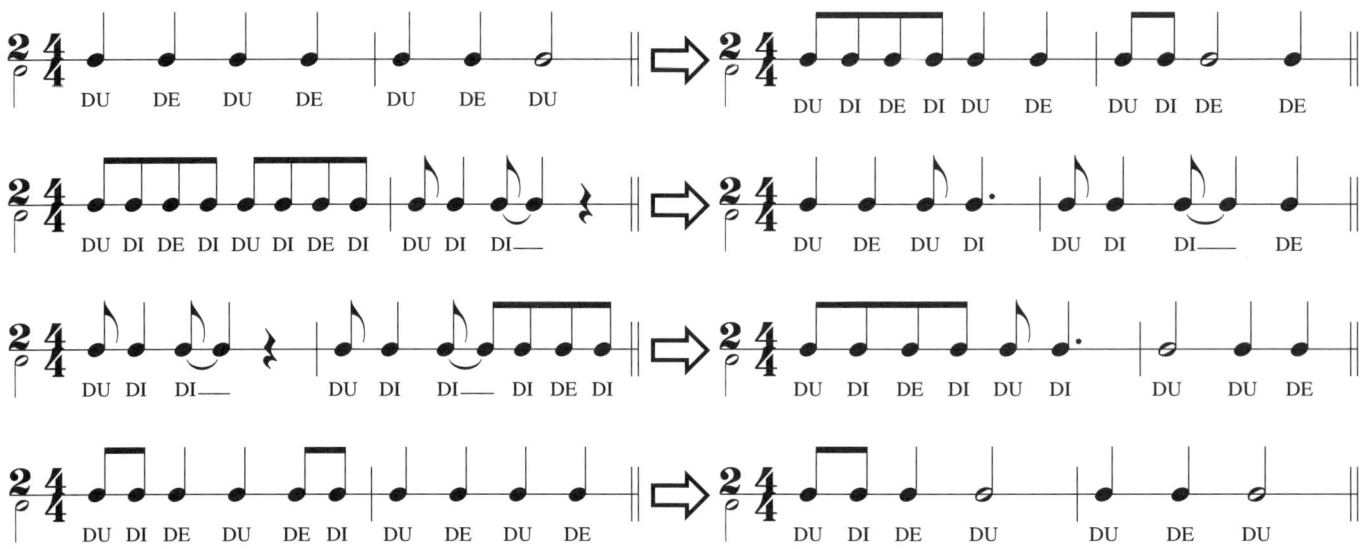

Unit 4 – "Simple Gifts"
Meter: Duple
Syllables: ♩ = DU; ♪ ♪ = DU DE; ♫♫ = DU TA DE TA

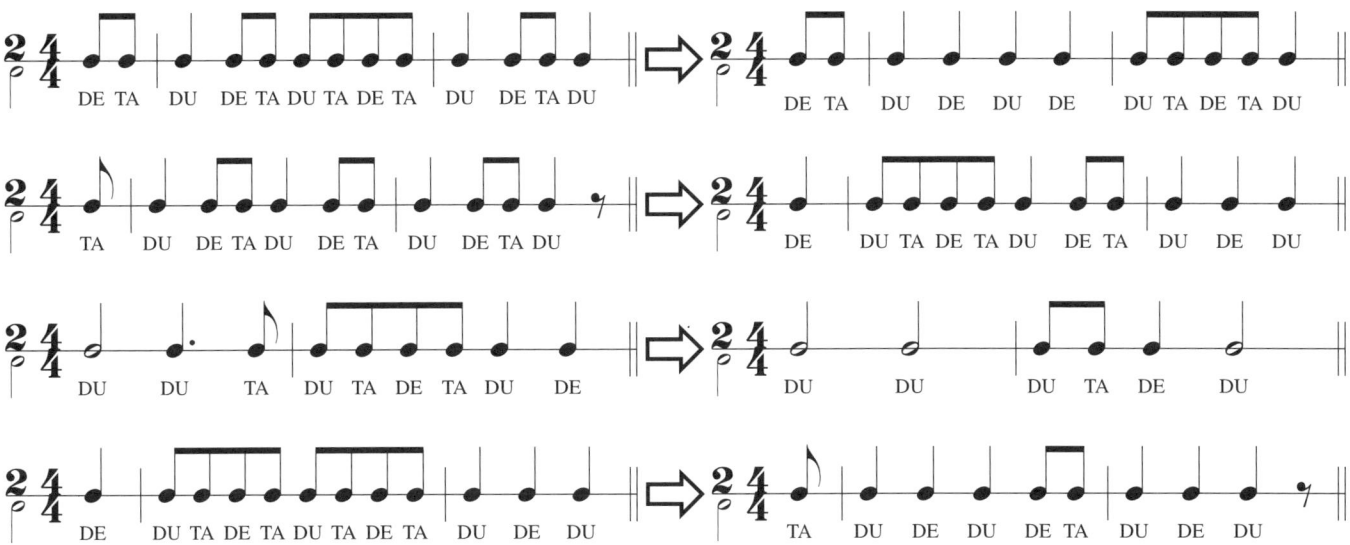

Unit 5 – "Down by the Riverside"
Meter: Duple (Swing Style)
Syllables: ♩ = DU; ♪ ♪ = DU DE; ♫♫ (swing) = DU DI DE DI

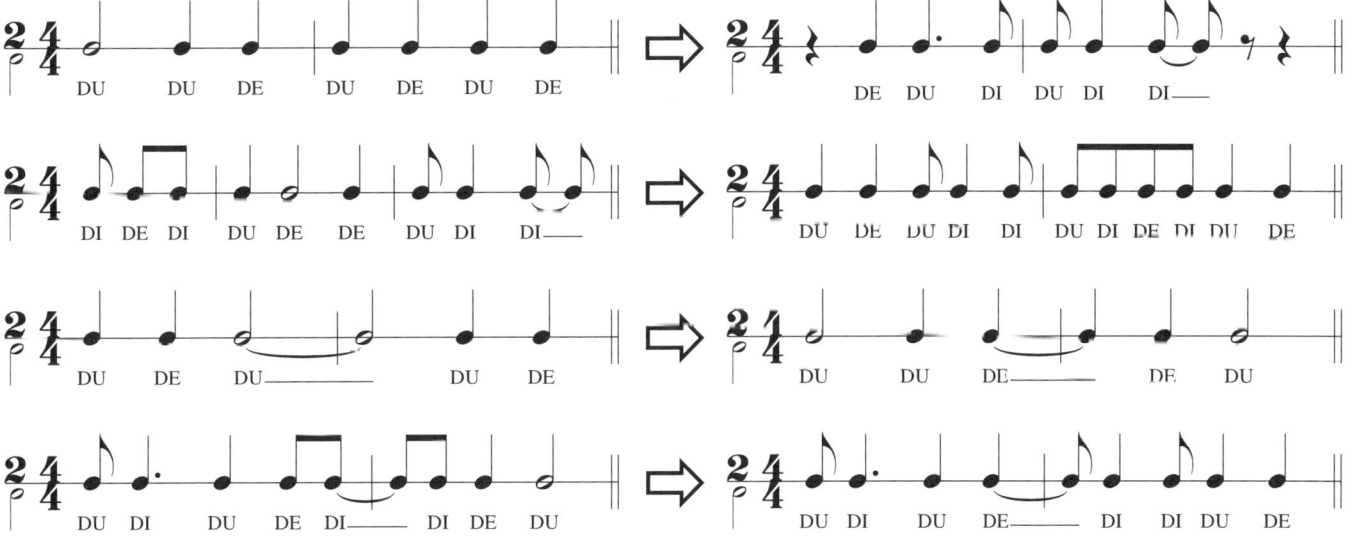

SOLFÈGE

Unit 1 – "Long, Long Ago"
Classification: Major – Tonic and Dominant
E♭ = DO (DO-based major; the arrow points to DO)
Syllables:

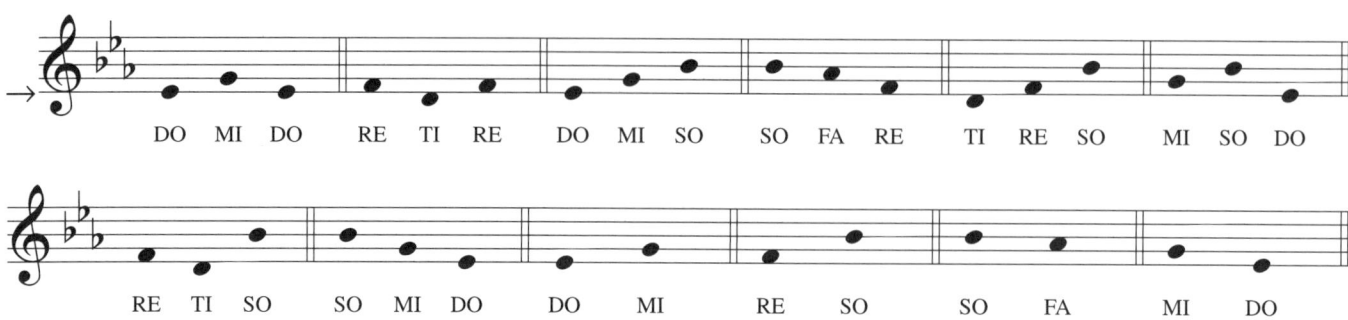

DO MI DO   RE TI RE   DO MI SO   SO FA RE   TI RE SO   MI SO DO

RE TI SO   SO MI DO   DO   MI   RE   SO   SO FA   MI   DO

Unit 2 – "Mary Ann"
Classification: Major – Tonic and Dominant
C = DO
Syllables:

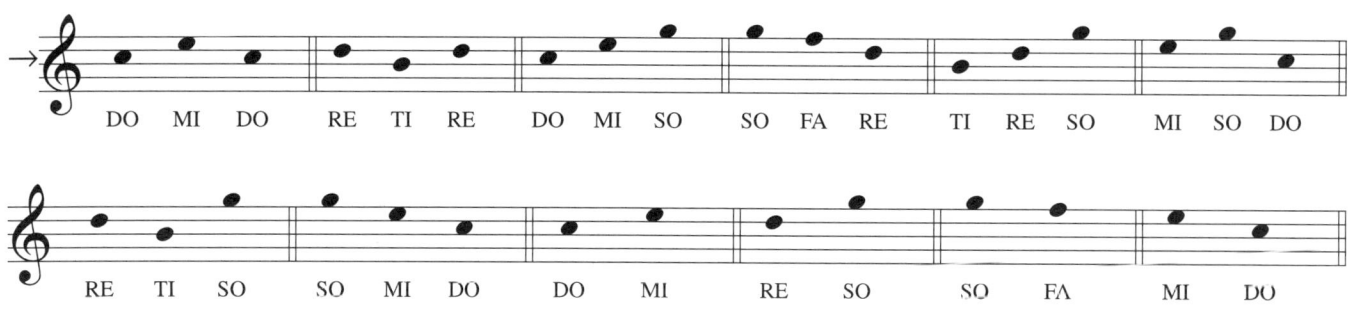

DO MI DO   RE TI RE   DO MI SO   SO FA RE   TI RE SO   MI SO DO

RE TI SO   SO MI DO   DO   MI   RE   SO   SO FA   MI   DO

Unit 3 – "Joshua"
Classification: Minor – Tonic and Dominant
D = LA (LA-based minor; the arrow points to DO)
Syllables:

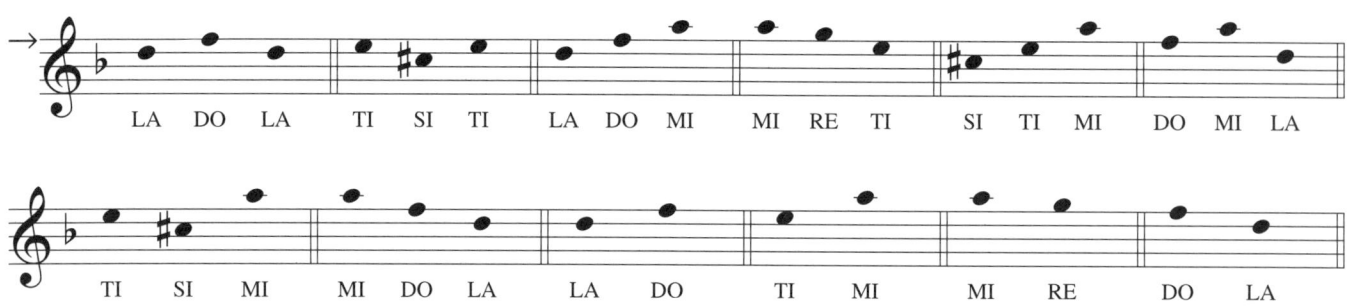

LA DO LA   TI SI TI   LA DO MI   MI RE TI   SI TI MI   DO MI LA

TI SI MI   MI DO LA   LA   DO   TI   MI   MI RE   DO   LA

Unit 4 – "Simple Gifts"

Classification: Major – Tonic, Subdominant, and Dominant

F = DO

Syllables:

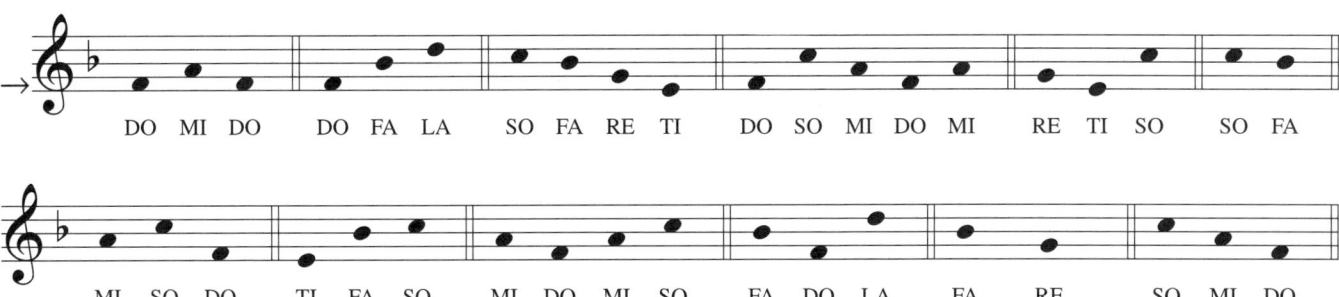

DO MI DO   DO FA LA   SO FA RE TI   DO SO MI DO MI   RE TI SO   SO FA

MI SO DO   TI FA SO   MI DO MI SO   FA DO LA   FA RE   SO MI DO

Unit 5 – "Down by the Riverside"

Classification: Major – Tonic, Subdominant, and Dominant

F = DO

Syllables:

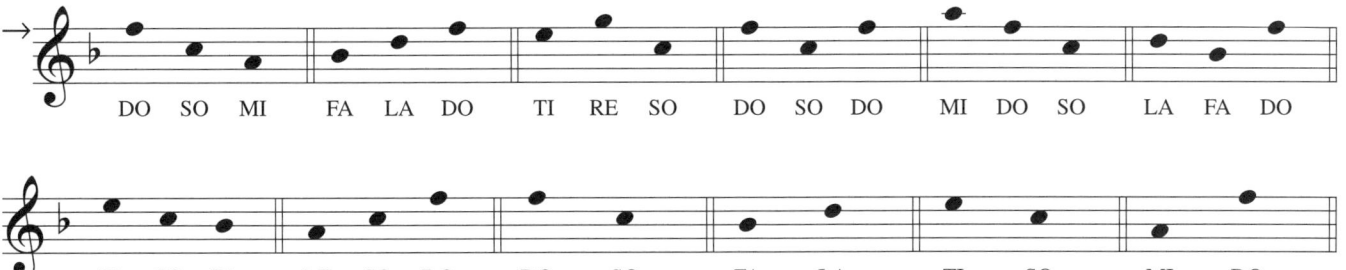

DO SO MI   FA LA DO   TI RE SO   DO SO DO   MI DO SO   LA FA DO

TI SO FA   MI SO DO   DO SO   FA LA   TI SO   MI DO

COMPACT DISC CONTENTS AND ASSIGNMENT SCHEDULE

CD 1

Track #	Page #	Assignment	Date
1	1, 9	Singing "Long, Long Ago"	
2	1, 9	Singing "Long, Long Ago" Neutral Syllable	
3	1, 9	"Long, Long Ago" Bass Line	
4	1, 9	"Long, Long Ago" Accompaniment	
5	1, 9	"Long, Long Ago" Melodic Patterns	
6	2–3	"Long, Long Ago" Rhythm Patterns – Neutral Syllable	
7	2–3	"Long, Long Ago" Rhythm Patterns – Rhythm Syllables	
8	2–3	"Long, Long Ago" Rhythm Patterns – Instrument	
9	3	"Long, Long Ago" Rhythm Phrases – Neutral Syllable	
10	3	"Long, Long Ago" Rhythm Phrases – Rhythm Syllables	
11	4–5	"Long, Long Ago" Tonal Patterns – Neutral Syllable	
12	4–5	"Long, Long Ago" Tonal Patterns – Solfège	
13	4–5	"Long, Long Ago" Tonal Patterns – Instrument	
14	6–7	Major – Tonic and Dominant Harmonic Progressions Concert E♭ Major – Neutral Syllable	
15	6–7	Major – Tonic and Dominant Harmonic Progressions Concert E♭ Major – Solfège	
16	8	"Long, Long Ago" Improvising Melodic Phrases – Example	
17	8	"Long, Long Ago" Improvising Melodic Phrases	
18	9	"Long, Long Ago" Improvise Rhythm Patterns to the Bass Line – Example	
19	12	"Long, Long Ago" Improvisation Skill 5 – Example 1	
20	12	"Long, Long Ago" Improvisation Skill 5 – Example 2	
21	12	"Long, Long Ago" Improvisation Skill 6 – Example	
22	13	"Long, Long Ago" Improvisation Skill 7 – Example	
23	13, 16	"Long, Long Ago" Melody and Improvisation – Trumpet	
24	9–16	"Long, Long Ago" Accompaniment – Concert E♭ Major	
25	17, 25	Singing "Mary Ann"	
26	17	"Mary Ann" Bass Line	
27	17	"Mary Ann" Accompaniment	
28	17	"Mary Ann" Melodic Patterns	
29	18	"Mary Ann" Rhythm Patterns – Neutral Syllable	
30	18	"Mary Ann" Rhythm Patterns – Rhythm Syllables	
31	19	"Mary Ann" Rhythm Phrases – Neutral Syllable	
32	19	"Mary Ann" Rhythm Phrases – Rhythm Syllables	
33	20–21	"Mary Ann" Tonal Patterns – Neutral Syllable	
34	20–21	"Mary Ann" Tonal Patterns – Solfège	
35	22–23	Major –Tonic and Dominant Harmonic Progressions Concert C Major – Neutral Syllable	
36	22–23	Major –Tonic and Dominant Harmonic Progressions Concert C Major – Solfège	
37	24	"Mary Ann" Improvising Melodic Phrases – Example	

UNIT I

PART I – REPERTOIRE

When first learning "Long, Long Ago," cover the notation.

1. LISTEN to "Long, Long Ago" – melody (CD 1, Tracks 1 and 2) and bass line (CD 1, Track 3).

2. With the accompaniment (CD 1, Track 4) SING the melody by ear with words and on a syllable such as "doo" and SING the bass line by ear on "doo."

3. PLAY your instrument by ear on the clicks immediately following each melodic pattern (CD 1, Track 5).

4. With the accompaniment (CD 1, Track 4) PLAY the melody and bass line on your instrument with the appropriate style of articulation. Personalize the tune using expressive phrasing, dynamics, and tonal and rhythmic variation.

> Long, Long Ago
> CD 1
> Tracks 1–5

Long, Long Ago

Thomas Haynes Bayly

Tell me the tales that to me were so dear, Long, long a-go, Long, long a-go;

Sing me the songs I de-light-ed to hear, Long, long a-go, long a-go.

Now you are here, all my grief is re-moved, Let me for-get that so long you have rov'd,

Let me be-lieve that you love as you loved, Long, long a-go, long a-go.

PART 2 – PATTERNS AND PROGRESSIONS

RHYTHM PATTERNS AND SERIES OF PATTERNS IN DUPLE METER

> Learn the patterns by ear – echo the patterns performed on the CD or by your teacher. When first learning the patterns, **cover the notation**.

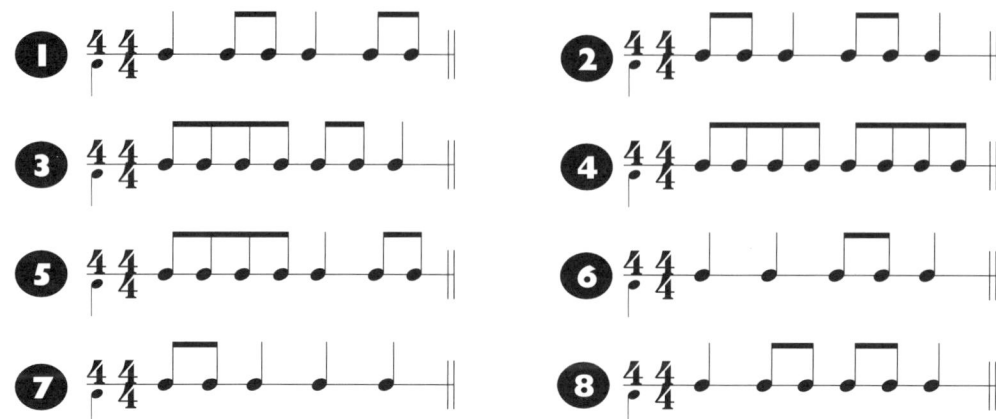

REPEAT AS NECESSARY

Echo Rhythm Patterns for "Long, Long Ago"

Learning these patterns is similar to learning words in a language. Becoming familiar with these patterns will improve your vocabulary for improvising rhythms to this tune.

Long, Long Ago CD 1 Tracks 6–8

1. ECHO the duple patterns on the syllable "bah" – CD 1, Track 6.

2. ECHO the patterns with rhythm syllables – CD 1, Track 7. The rhythm syllables will help you to organize and remember the patterns. See page vii for more information on rhythm syllables.

3. ECHO the patterns on your instrument on E♭–DO. Use the style(s) of articulation appropriate for "Long, Long Ago." CD 1, Track 8.

MACROBEAT: The paired large beats that are felt in the music.

MICROBEAT: The small beats that are felt in the music.

DUPLE METER: A usual meter in which there are two microbeats for every macrobeat.

The number (4) tells how many macrobeats (DU) are in the measure. The symbol (♩) indicates what kind of note is a macrobeat (DU). (♩=DU; ♫=DU DE)

Improvise Rhythm Patterns for "Long, Long Ago"

Now that you are familiar with the rhythm patterns on CD 1, Tracks 6, 7, and 8, improvise patterns using the rhythm vocabulary that you have learned.

1. Listen to the rhythm patterns performed on CD 1, Track 6. After each pattern IMPROVISE a different pattern using the syllable "bah."

2. Listen to the rhythm patterns performed on CD 1, Track 7. After each pattern IMPROVISE a different pattern using macrobeats and microbeats with rhythm syllables. (DU, DU DE)

3. Improvise patterns on your instrument on E♭–DO. Use the style(s) of articulation appropriate for "Long, Long Ago." CD 1, Track 8.

Example:

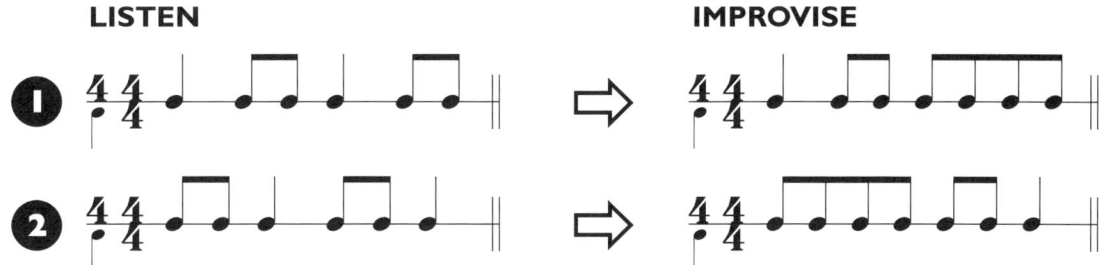

Continue with rhythm patterns 3 through 8 (CD 1, Tracks 6–8).

Echo and Improvise Series of Rhythm Patterns in Duple Meter

Improvising a series of patterns is similar to speaking a sentence or phrase in language.

1. ECHO the two-measure rhythm phrases using the syllable "bah" (CD 1, Track 9), with rhythm syllables (CD 1, Track 10), and with your instrument on E♭-DO (CD 1, Track 9 or 10).

2. After each rhythm phrase, IMPROVISE a different phrase, using the syllable "bah" (CD 1, Track 9), with rhythm syllables (CD 1, Track 10), and with your instrument (CD 1, Track 9 or 10).

The number (4) tells how many macrobeats (DU) are in the measure. The symbol (♩) indicates what kind of note is a macrobeat (DU). (♩=DU; ♫=DU DE)

> **Long, Long Ago**
> **CD 1**
> **Tracks 9–10**

Example:

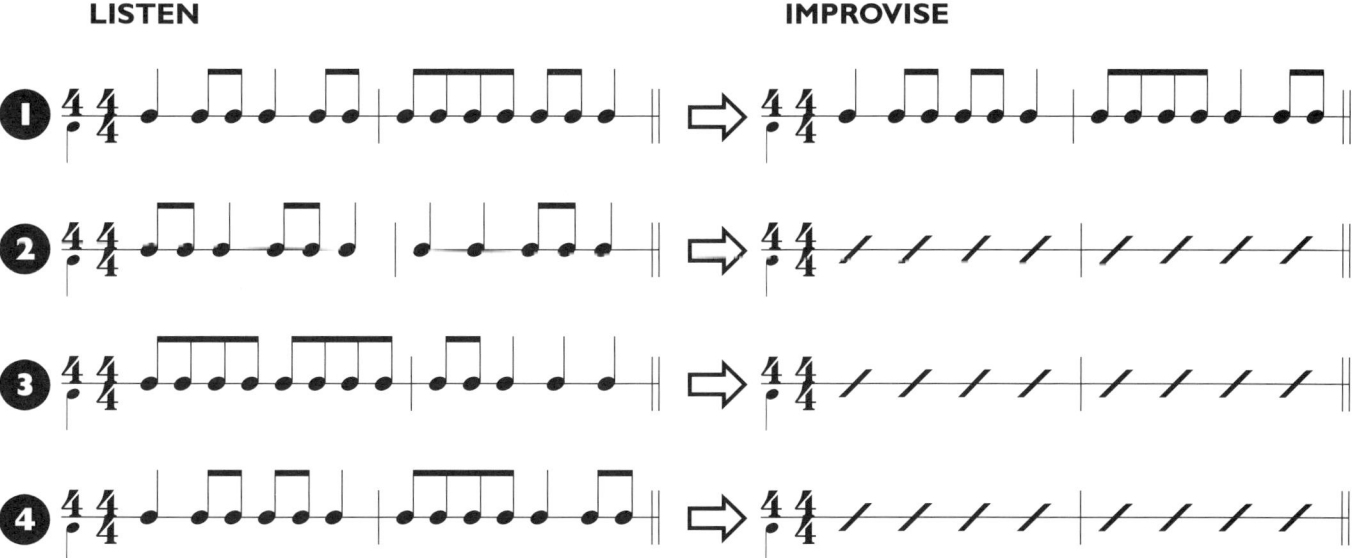

REPEAT AS NECESSARY

TONAL PATTERNS AND HARMONIC PROGRESSIONS

You have learned to improvise rhythm patterns and phrases of rhythm patterns. Now learn to improvise tonal patterns and harmonic progressions. Improve your tonal vocabulary by learning the following tonal patterns, first with a neutral syllable and then with solfège.

Learn the patterns by ear – echo the patterns performed on the CD or by your teacher. When first learning the patterns, **cover the notation**.

Echo Tonal Patterns for "Long, Long Ago"

(E♭ Major – Tonic and Dominant)

Establish Tonality (Concert Pitch)

Long, Long Ago CD 1 Tracks 11–13

1. ECHO, singing the following patterns on the syllable "bum" (CD 1, Track 11).

2. ECHO, singing the following patterns with solfège (CD 1, Track 12).

3. ECHO, playing each of the following patterns on your instrument (Track 13).

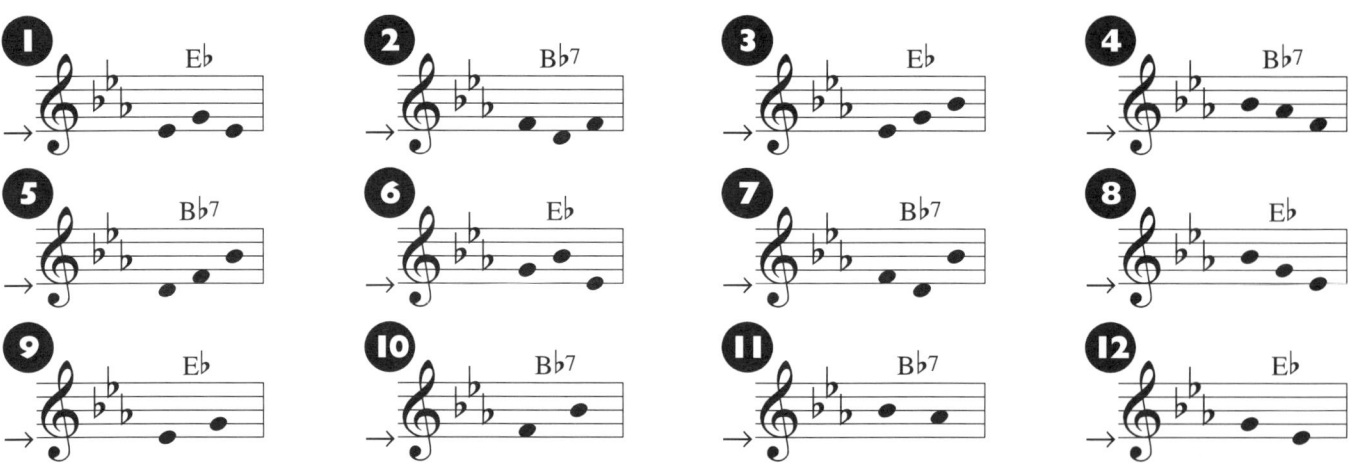

REPEAT AS NECESSARY

SING the Root (DO or SO) and NAME the Function (Tonic or Dominant) in E♭ Major.

Long, Long Ago CD 1 Track 12

1. LISTEN to the tonal patterns performed on CD 1, Track 12. After each pattern, SING the root of that function using tonal syllables, and immediately identify the harmonic function. SING: "DO" and "Tonic" or "SO" and "Dominant." (E♭=Tonic; B♭7=Dominant)

2. LISTEN again to CD 1, Track 12, and PLAY the roots on your instrument.

TONIC: In major tonality, any combination of DO, MI, SO.

DOMINANT: In major tonality, any combination of SO, FA, RE, TI.

MAJOR TONALITY: The resting tone is DO.

4

E♭ indicates TONIC function and B♭7 indicates DOMINANT function. A TONIC pattern in major tonality includes any combination of "DO MI SO" and a DOMINANT pattern includes any combination of "SO FA RE TI."

SOLFÈGE SHOULD ALWAYS BE SUNG–NOT SPOKEN
(See page vii for an explanation of solfège.)

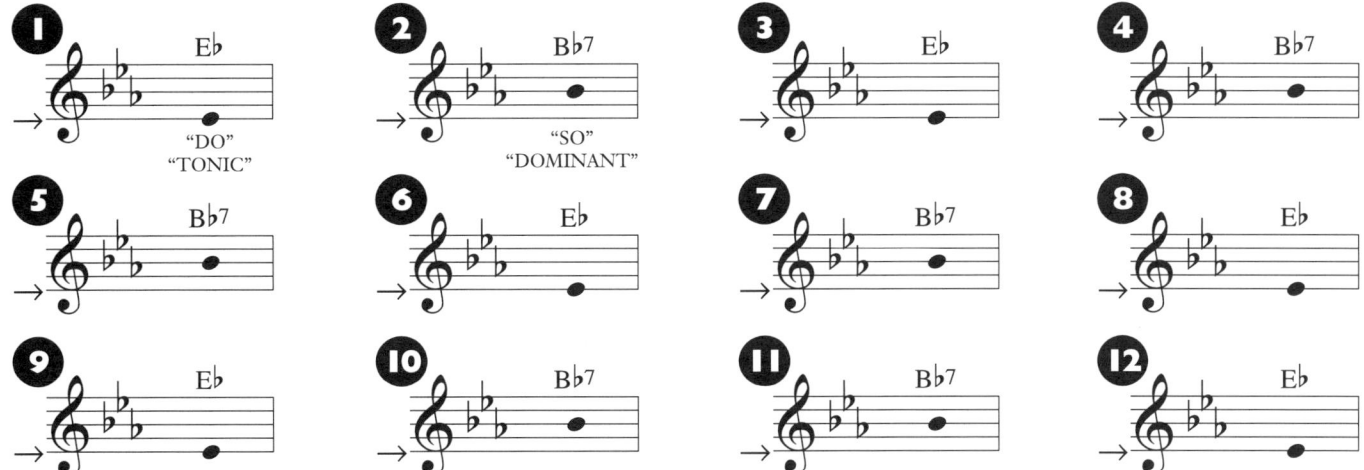

REPEAT AS NECESSARY

Improvise Tonal Patterns for "Long, Long Ago"
(Tonic and Dominant Functions in E♭ Major)

1. LISTEN again to the tonal patterns performed on CD 1, Tracks 11, 12, and 13.

2. After each pattern, IMPROVISE a different pattern with the same harmonic function with a neutral syllable ("bum" – CD 1, Track 11).

3. After each pattern, IMPROVISE a different pattern with the same harmonic function with solfège (CD 1, Track 12).

4. After each pattern, IMPROVISE a different pattern with the same harmonic function on your instrument (CD 1, Track 13).

Long, Long Ago
CD 1
Tracks 11–13

Example:

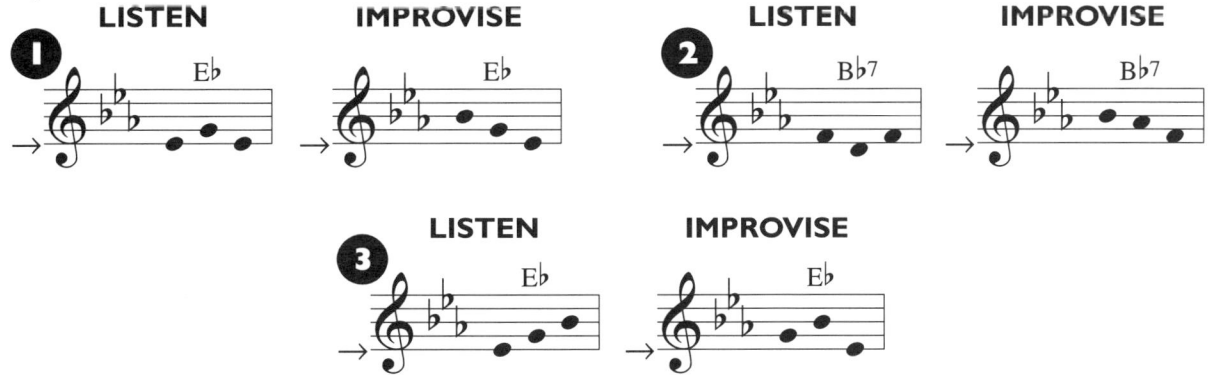

5

ECHO and IMPROVISE Series of Tonic and Dominant Patterns in E♭ Major

Long, Long Ago
CD 1
Tracks 14–15

Improvising a series of patterns to make a harmonic progression in music is similar to speaking a sentence or phrase in language. **Anticipate** and **predict** the harmonic progression. Where does the harmony go and where might it go?

1. Using the syllable "bum," ECHO (SING) the series of patterns (CD 1, Track 14).

2. Using solfège, ECHO (SING) the series of patterns (CD 1, Track 15).

3. ECHO the series of patterns on your instrument (CD 1, Track 14 or 15).

4. After each series of patterns, SING the bass line (roots) using solfège (CD 1, Track 15).

5. After each series of patterns, PLAY the bass line (roots) on your instrument (CD 1, Track 14 or 15).

6. After each series of patterns, IMPROVISE a different series of patterns over the same harmonic progression using solfège (CD 1, Track 15); with a neutral syllable ("bum" – CD 1, Track 14); and on your instrument (CD 1, Track 14 or 15).

Example:

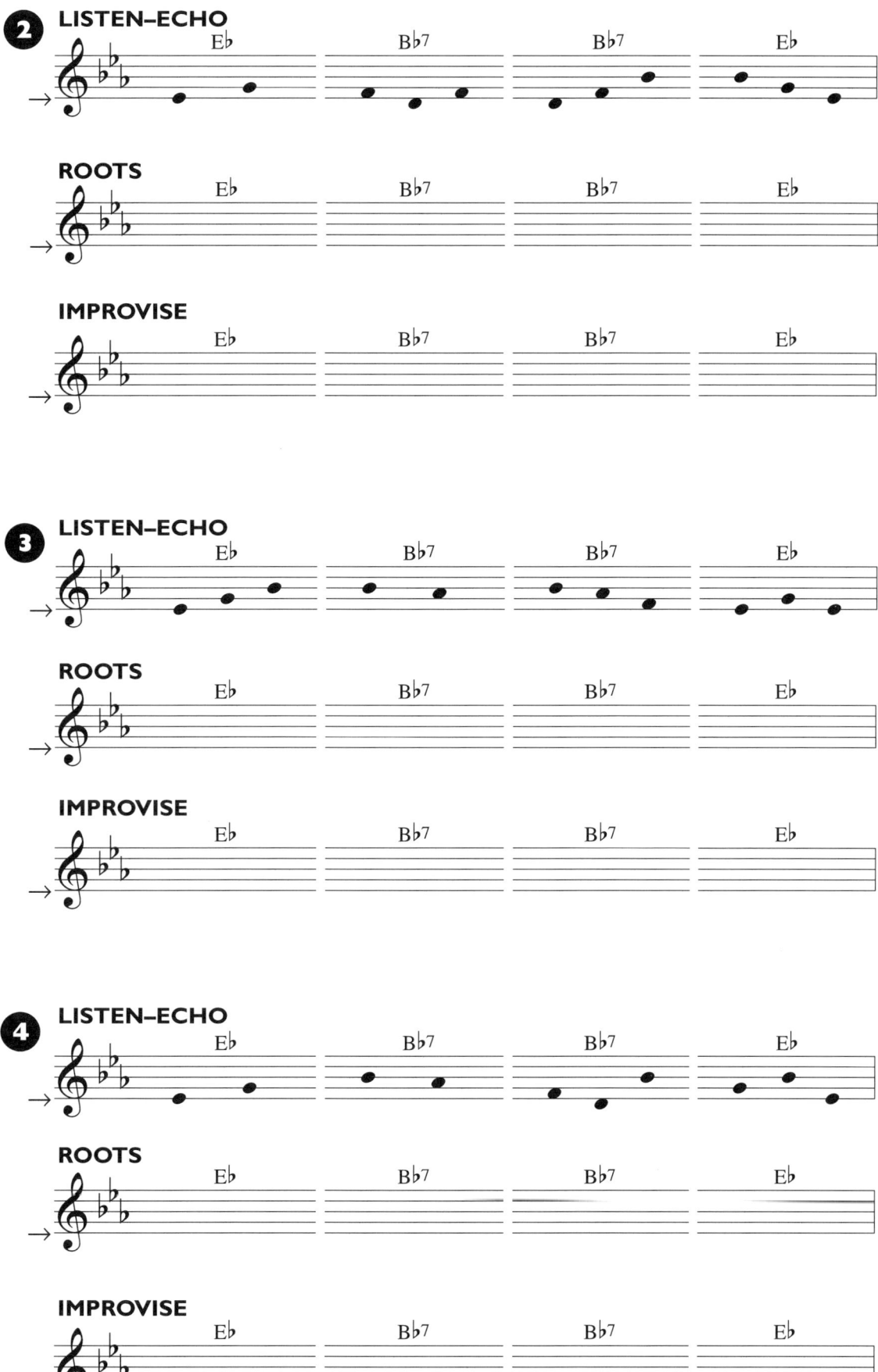

PART 3 – IMPROVISING MELODIC PHRASES

Sing improvised melodies to familiar repertoire.

Long,
Long Ago
CD 1
Track 16

1. Listen to CD 1, Track 16. The performer sings the first phrase (antecedent phrase) of "Long, Long Ago"; instead of continuing with the original second phrase (consequent phrase), you hear an improvised melody that continues the harmonic progression. Listen to all four antecedent phrases and improvised consequent phrases.

Example:

Long, Long Ago

Long,
Long Ago
CD 1
Track 17

2. Listen to CD 1, Track 17. After hearing the first phrase (antecedent phrase) of "Long, Long Ago," continue the harmonic progression of the tune and sing a second phrase (consequent phrase) that is different from the original melody. Continue in a similar manner with the remaining phrases. Direct your melody toward chord tones, e.g., "DO," "MI," "SO" (CD 1, Track 17).

3. Perform in a similar manner on your instrument (CD 1, Track 17).

Now, you try:

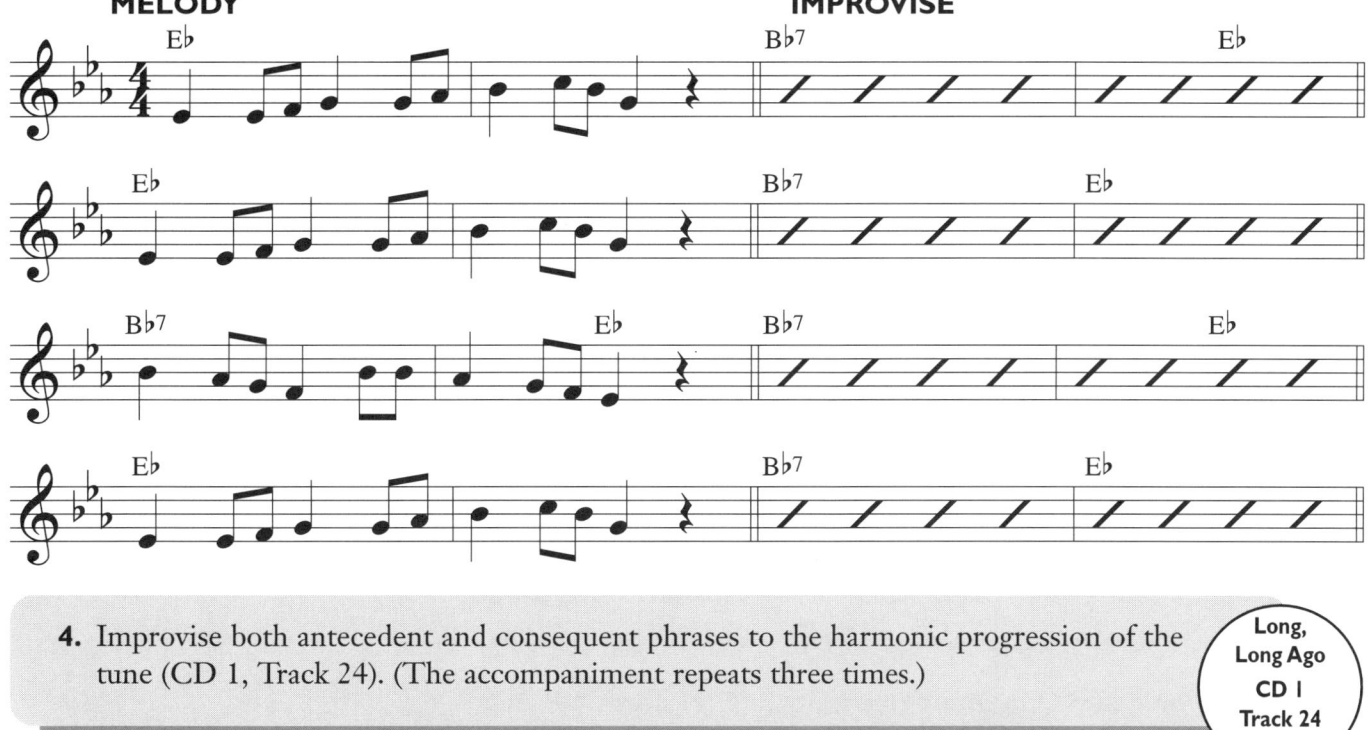

4. Improvise both antecedent and consequent phrases to the harmonic progression of the tune (CD 1, Track 24). (The accompaniment repeats three times.)

Long, Long Ago
CD 1
Track 24

PART 4 – LEARNING TO IMPROVISE
TONALLY   RHYTHMICALLY   EXPRESSIVELY

SEVEN SKILLS

Before you begin the Seven Skills, review "Long, Long Ago" (CD 1, Tracks 1–5)

1. SING and PLAY the melody.

2. SING and PLAY the bass line (roots).

Long, Long Ago
CD 1
Tracks 1–5, 18

Skill 1

1. Listen to CD 1, Track 18. The performer improvises rhythm patterns to the bass line of "Long, Long Ago."

Example:

9

Long, Long Ago CD 1 Track 24

2. Improvise rhythm patterns to the bass line of "Long, Long Ago." SING your improvisation with the neutral syllable "doo," and then PLAY it on your instrument (CD 1, Track 24).

Skill 2

1. Establish tonality in E♭ major and SING each of the four parts below for the harmonic functions of "Long, Long Ago." For example, SING "DO, SO, DO" – "DO, TI, DO" – "MI, FA, MI" – "SO, SO, SO."

2. Play each part on your instrument.

When in a group setting, each student should select a part to sing and play for Skills 3 and 4. When performing alone, start with the bass line (chord roots – Skill 1) and then be sure to perform Skills 3 and 4 using the other three parts as well.

Example of Tonic and Dominant Harmony in E♭ Major – 4 Parts:

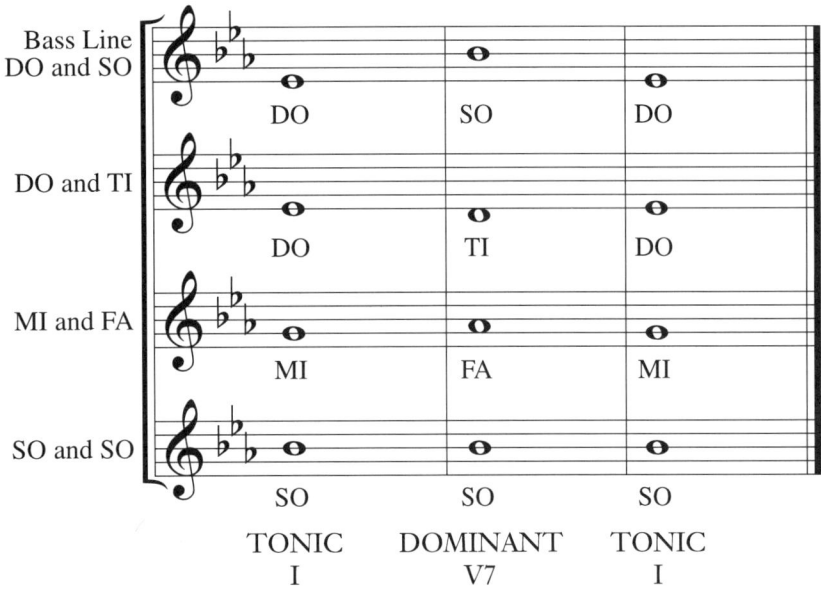

Skill 3

Long, Long Ago CD 1 Track 24

Learn the harmonic rhythm for "Long, Long Ago" using the pitches from the harmony in **Skill 2**. SING every part. PLAY these parts on your instrument (CD 1, Track 24).

Skill 4

Using a neutral syllable (e.g., "doo"), improvise rhythm patterns to the harmonic progression using pitches learned in Skill 2 (#2, 3, 4, and 5, on the facing page). Select a part and improvise rhythm patterns. Do this with each part. Interact with the melody (#1) and other parts (CD 1, Track 24). First SING, then PLAY these parts on your instrument. Listen to CD 1, Track 18 for an example using the bass line.

Long, Long Ago

MELODY

BASS LINE; IMPROVISE RHYTHM

IMPROVISE RHYTHM ON "DO" AND "TI"

IMPROVISE RHYTHM ON "MI" AND "FA"

IMPROVISE RHYTHM ON "SO"

Long,
Long Ago
CD 1
Tracks 19–20

I. Listen to CD 1, Tracks 19 and 20. The performer improvises tonal patterns to the harmonic progression using macrobeats. In the first example (CD 1, Track 19), ♩=macrobeat. In the second example (CD 1, Track 20), ♩=macrobeat.

Example 1: (♩ = DU)

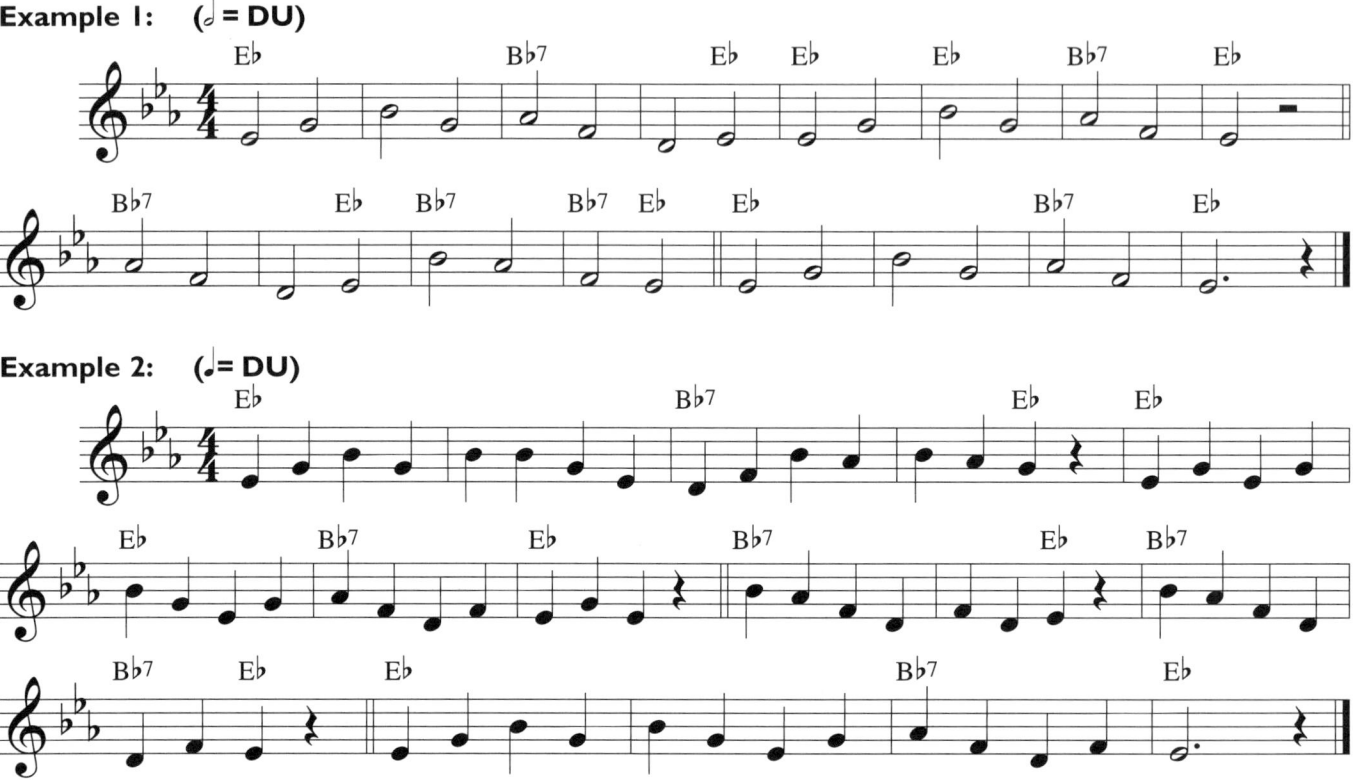

Example 2: (♩ = DU)

2. Using macrobeats improvise (SING, then PLAY on your instrument) tonal patterns to the harmonic progression (CD 1, Track 24).

Long,
Long Ago
CD 1
Tracks 21,
24

Skill 6

I. Listen to CD 1, Track 21. The performer improvises tonal patterns and rhythm patterns to the harmonic progression.

Example:

2. Improvise (SING, then PLAY on your instrument) tonal patterns and rhythm patterns to the harmonic progression (CD 1, Track 24).

Long, Long Ago
CD 1
Tracks 22, 24

Skill 7

1. Listen to CD 1, Track 22. The performer improvises by decorating and embellishing the melodic material in **Skill 6**.

Example:

2. Decorate and embellish the melodic material in Skill 6. Improvise melodies to the harmonic progression (CD 1, Track 24). Learn to SING and PLAY the solos provided (CD 1, Track 23).

IMPROVISE to "Long, Long Ago" (CD 1, Track 24). Suggestions for developing meaningful improvisations are found on page v.

PART 5 – READING AND WRITING

Rhythm Writing

1. Write the patterns on page 2 or notate improvised patterns. Establish meter and remember to group the notes into patterns and phrases before writing them.

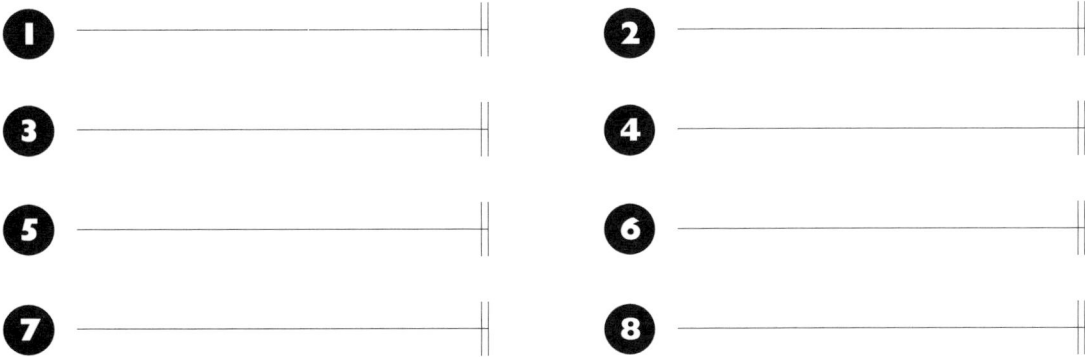

2. Write the series of patterns on page 3 or notate an improvised series of patterns.

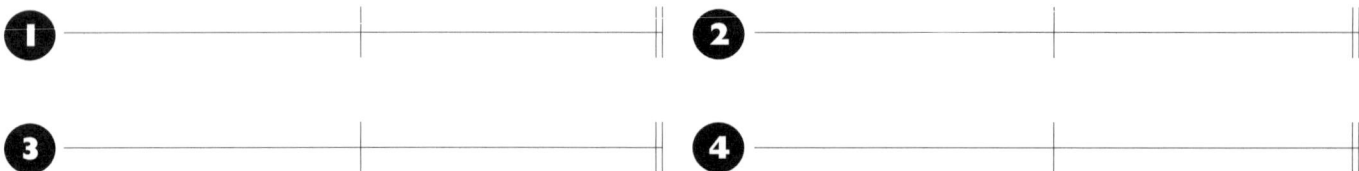

Tonal Writing

1. Write the patterns on page 4 or notate improvised patterns. Establish tonality and remember to group the notes into patterns and phrases before writing them.

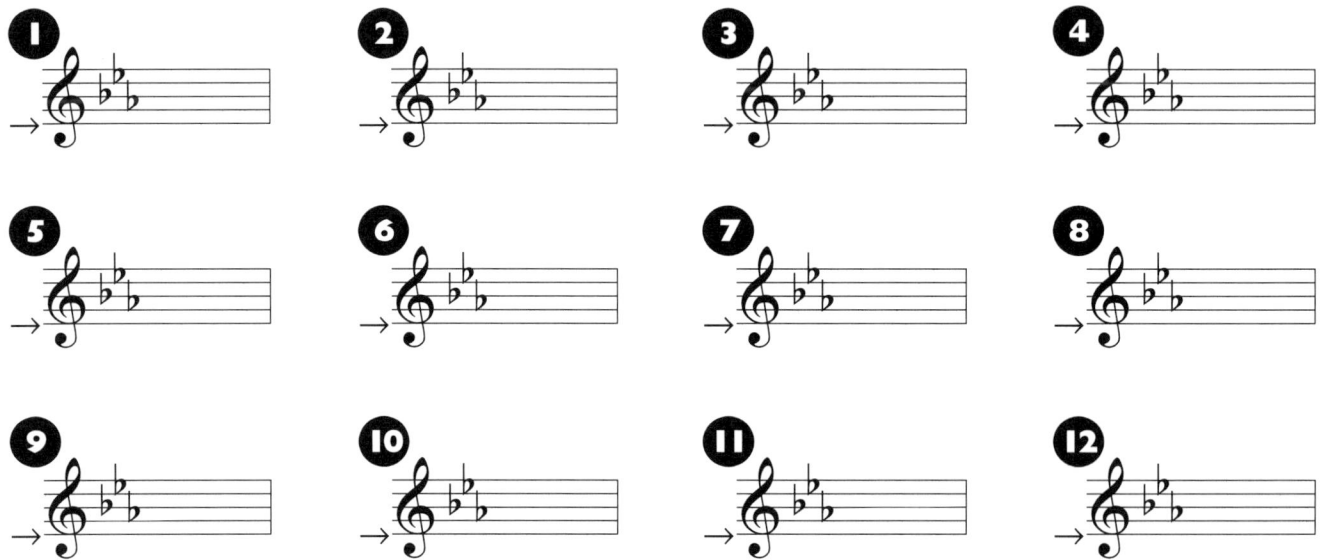

2. Write the series of patterns on pages 6–7 or notate an improvised series of patterns for the progression.

IMPROVISE – READ – COMPOSE

READ "Long, Long Ago" and IMPROVISE to the harmonic progression. SING and PLAY the melody and/or bass line on your instrument (CD 1, Track 24). Also, COMPOSE other melodies using the harmonic progression indicated and the tonal and rhythm vocabulary that you have learned.

Long, Long Ago

Listen to CD 1, Track 23. The performer plays an interpretation of the melody followed by an improvised solo. Learn to sing and play the solo performed on the CD. Use the space provided to finish transcribing the solo on CD 1, Track 23, or to notate other solos. Analyze the solos for vocabulary and ideas to incorporate into your own improvised solos. See page v for suggestions about developing meaningful improvisations. Perform with the accompaniment on CD 1, Track 24.

Long, Long Ago
CD 1
Tracks 23–24

Long, Long Ago

PART 1 – REPERTOIRE

When first learning "Mary Ann," cover the notation.

1. LISTEN to "Mary Ann" – melody (CD 1, Track 25) and bass line (CD 1, Track 26).

2. With the accompaniment (CD 1, Track 27) SING the melody by ear with words and on a syllable such as "doo" and SING the bass line by ear on "doo."

3. PLAY your instrument by ear on the clicks immediately following each melodic pattern (CD 1, Track 28).

4. With the accompaniment (CD 1, Track 27) PLAY the melody and bass line on your instrument with the appropriate style of articulation. Personalize the tune using expressive phrasing, dynamics, and tonal and rhythmic variation.

Mary Ann
CD 1
Tracks 25–28

Mary Ann

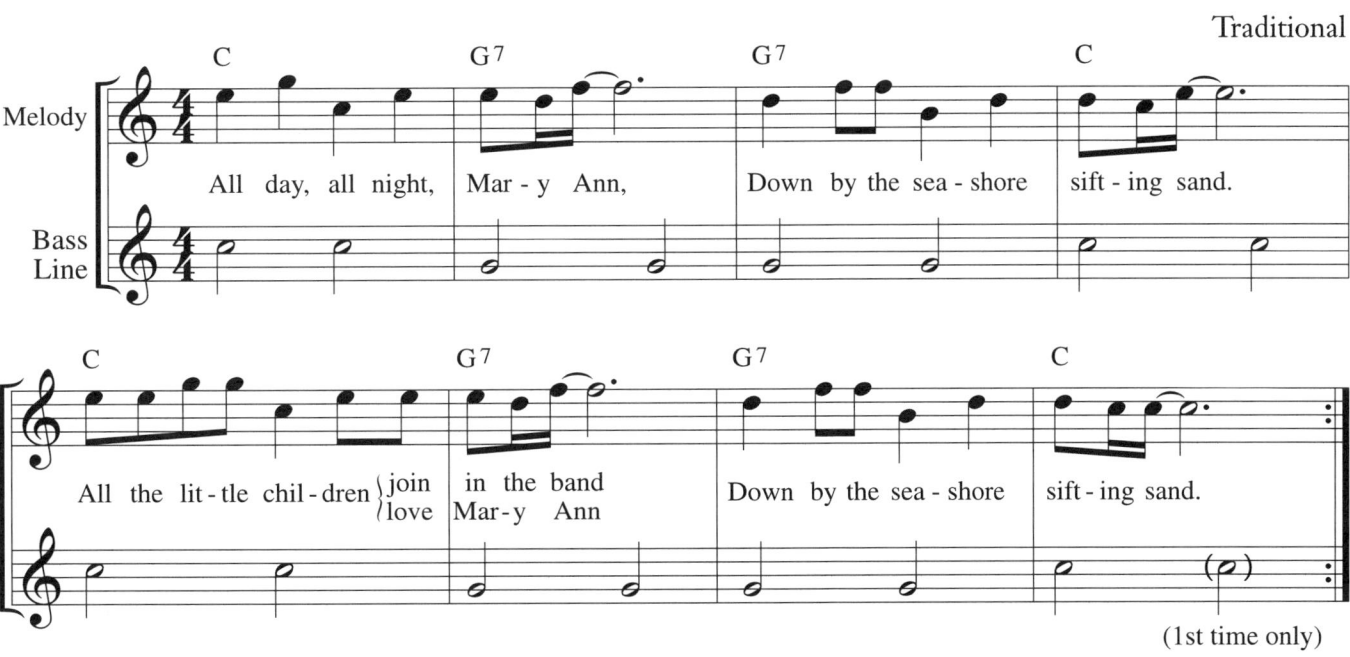

Traditional

(1st time only)

PART 2 – PATTERNS AND PROGRESSIONS

RHYTHM PATTERNS AND SERIES OF PATTERNS IN DUPLE METER (Latin Style)

Learn the patterns by ear – echo the patterns performed on the CD or by your teacher. When first learning the patterns, **cover the notation**.

Echo Rhythm Patterns for "Mary Ann"

**Mary Ann
CD 1
Tracks 29–30**

Learning these patterns is similar to learning words in a language. Becoming familiar with these patterns will improve your vocabulary for improvising rhythms to this tune.

1. ECHO the duple patterns on the syllable "bah" – CD 1, Track 29.

2. ECHO the patterns with rhythm syllables – CD 1, Track 30. The rhythm syllables will help you to organize and remember the patterns. See page vii for more information on rhythm syllables.

3. ECHO the patterns on your instrument on C–DO. Use the style(s) of articulation appropriate for "Mary Ann." CD 1, Track 29 or 30.

The number (4) tells how many macrobeats (DU) are in a measure. The symbol (♩) indicates what kind of note is a macrobeat (DU). (♩ =DU; ♫ =DU DE)

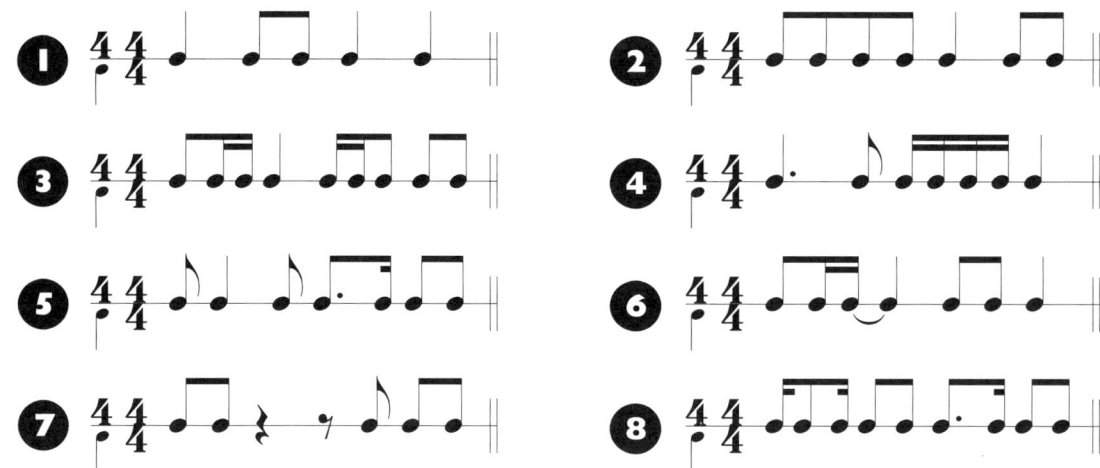

REPEAT AS NECESSARY

Improvise Rhythm Patterns for "Mary Ann"

Now that you are familiar with the rhythm patterns on CD 1, Tracks 29 and 30, improvise patterns using the rhythm vocabulary that you have learned.

**Mary Ann
CD 1
Tracks 29–30**

1. Listen to the rhythm patterns performed on CD 1, Track 29. After each pattern IMPROVISE a different pattern using the syllable "bah."

2. Listen to the rhythm patterns performed on CD 1, Track 30. After each pattern IMPROVISE a different pattern using rhythm syllables.

3. IMPROVISE patterns on your instrument on C–DO. Use the style(s) of articulation appropriate for "Mary Ann." CD 1, Track 29 or 30.

The number (4) tells how many macrobeats (DU) are in a measure. The symbol (♩) indicates what kind of note is a macrobeat (DU). (♩ =DU; ♫ =DU DE)

Example:

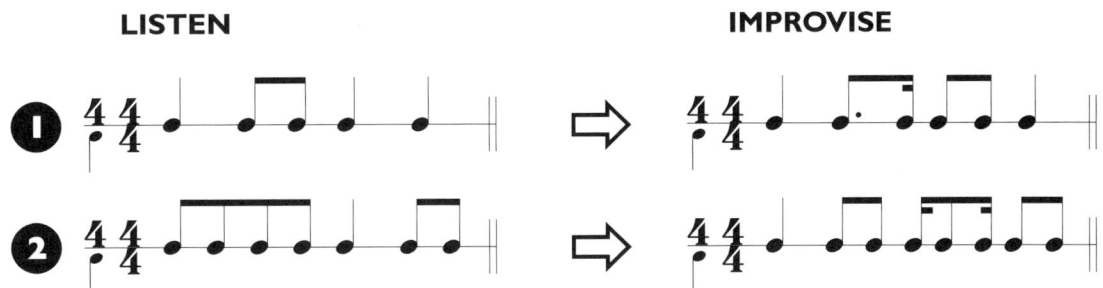

LISTEN   IMPROVISE

Continue with rhythm patterns 3 through 8 (CD 1, Tracks 29–30).

Echo and Improvise Series of Rhythm Patterns in Duple Meter

Improvising a series of patterns is like speaking a sentence or phrase in language.

1. ECHO rhythm phrases using the syllable "bah" (CD 1, Track 31), with rhythm syllables (CD 1, Track 32), and with your instrument on C–DO (CD 1, Track 31 or 32).

2. After each rhythm phrase, IMPROVISE a different phrase using the syllable "bah" (CD 1, Track 31), with rhythm syllables (CD 1, Track 32), and with your instrument (CD 1, Track 31 or 32).

The number (4) tells how many macrobeats (DU) are in a measure.
The symbol (♩) indicates what kind of note is a macrobeat (DU). (♩=DU; ♫=DU DE)

Mary Ann
CD 1
Tracks 31–32

LISTEN   IMPROVISE
(Example)

REPEAT AS NECESSARY

TONAL PATTERNS AND HARMONIC PROGRESSIONS

You have just learned to improvise rhythm patterns and phrases of rhythm patterns. Now learn to improvise tonal patterns and harmonic progressions. Improve your tonal vocabulary by learning the following tonal patterns, first with a neutral syllable and then with solfège.

> Learn the patterns by ear – echo the patterns performed on the CD or by your teacher. When first learning the patterns, **cover the notation**.

Echo Tonal Patterns for "Mary Ann"

Establish Tonality (Concert Pitch)

(C Major – Tonic and Dominant)

Mary Ann CD 1 Tracks 33–34

1. ECHO, singing the following patterns on the syllable "bum" (CD 1, Track 33).

2. ECHO, singing the following patterns with solfège (CD 1, Track 34).

3. ECHO, playing each of the following patterns on your instrument (CD 1, Track 33 or 34).

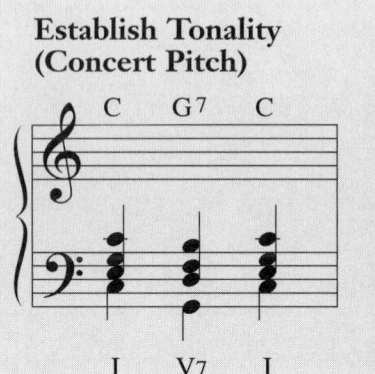

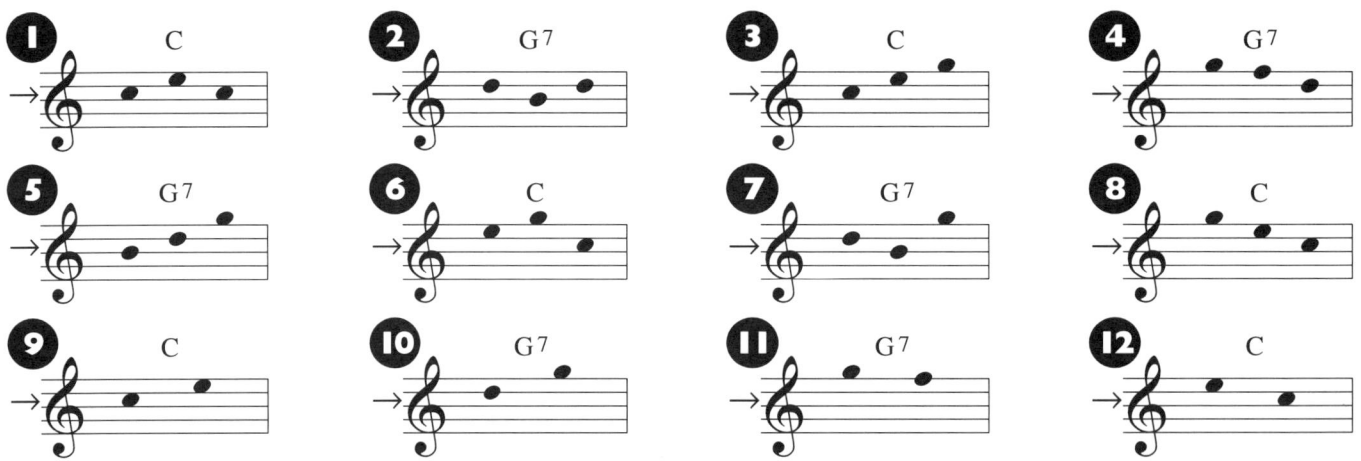

REPEAT AS NECESSARY

SING the Root (DO or SO) and NAME the Function (Tonic or Dominant) in C Major

Mary Ann CD 1 Track 34

1. LISTEN to the tonal patterns performed on CD 1, Track 34. After each pattern, SING the root of that function using tonal syllables, and immediately identify the harmonic function. SING: "DO" and "Tonic," or "SO" and "Dominant." (C=Tonic; G7=Dominant)

2. LISTEN again to CD 1, Track 34, and PLAY the roots on your instrument.

20

C indicates TONIC function and G7 indicates DOMINANT function. A TONIC pattern in major tonality includes any combination of "DO MI SO" and a DOMINANT pattern includes any combination of "SO FA RE TI."

SOLFÈGE SHOULD ALWAYS BE SUNG–NOT SPOKEN

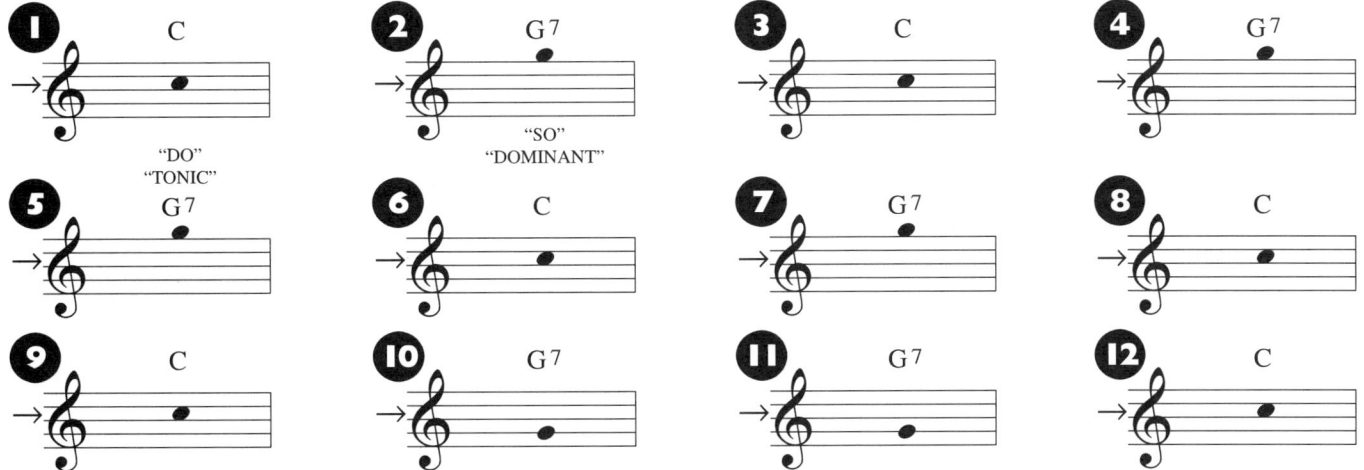

REPEAT AS NECESSARY

Improvise Tonal Patterns for "Mary Ann" (Tonic and Dominant Functions in C Major)

1. LISTEN again to the tonal patterns performed on CD 1, Tracks 33 and 34.

2. After each pattern, IMPROVISE a different pattern with the same harmonic function with a neutral syllable ("bum" – CD 1, Track 33).

3. After each pattern, IMPROVISE a different pattern with the same harmonic function with solfège (CD 1, Track 34).

4. After each pattern, IMPROVISE a different pattern with the same harmonic function on your instrument (CD 1, Track 33 or 34).

Mary Ann
CD 1
Tracks 33–34

Example:

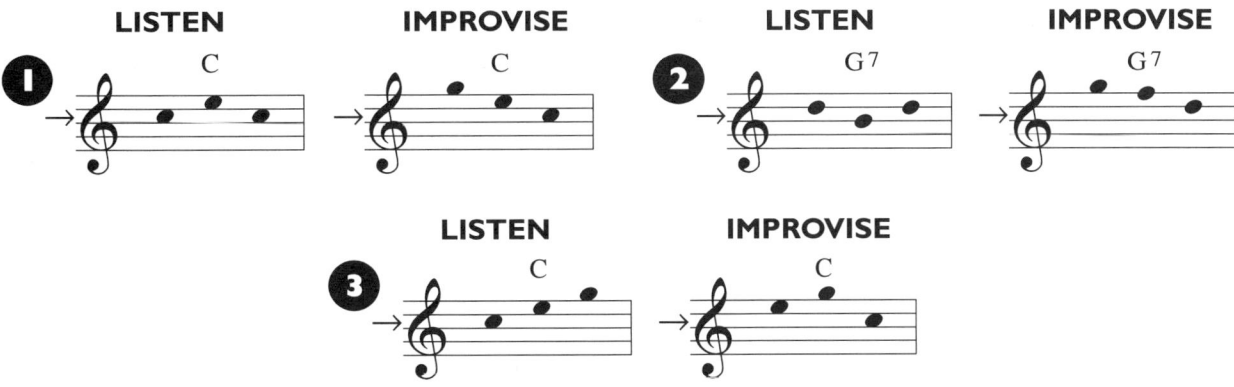

Continue with tonal patterns 4 through 12 (CD 1, Tracks 33–34).

21

ECHO and IMPROVISE Series of Tonic and Dominant Patterns in C Major

Improvising a series of patterns to make a harmonic progression in music is like speaking a sentence or phrase in language. **Anticipate** and **predict** the harmonic progression. Where does the harmony go and where might it go?

Mary Ann
CD 1
Tracks 35–36

1. Using the syllable "bum," ECHO (SING) the series of patterns (CD 1, Track 35).

2. Using solfège, ECHO (SING) the series of patterns (CD 1, Track 36).

3. ECHO the series of patterns on your instrument (CD 1, Track 35 or 36).

4. After each series of patterns, SING the bass line (roots) using solfège (CD 1, Track 36).

5. After each series of patterns, PLAY the bass line (roots) on your instrument (CD 1, Track 35 or 36).

6. After each series of patterns, IMPROVISE a different series of patterns over the same harmonic progression using solfège (CD 1, Track 36), with a neutral syllable ("bum" – CD 1, Track 35), and on your instrument (CD 1, Track 35 or 36).

Example:

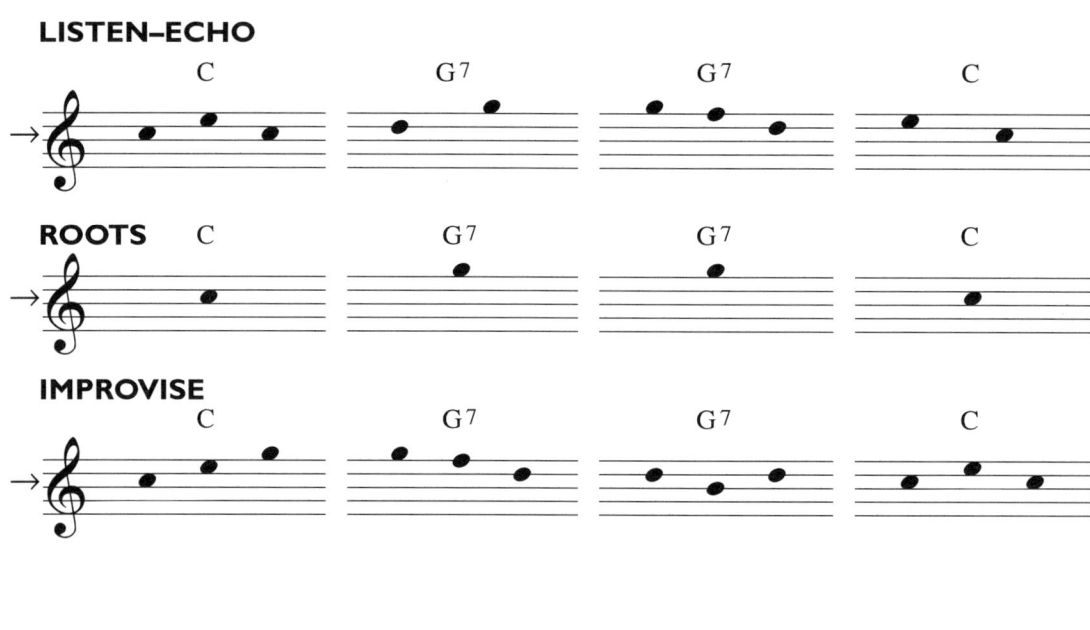

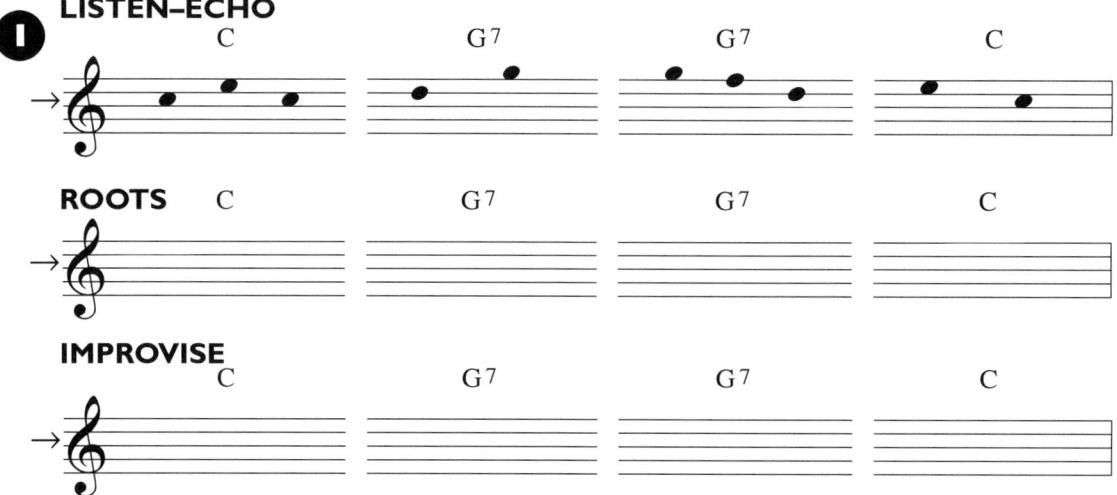

22

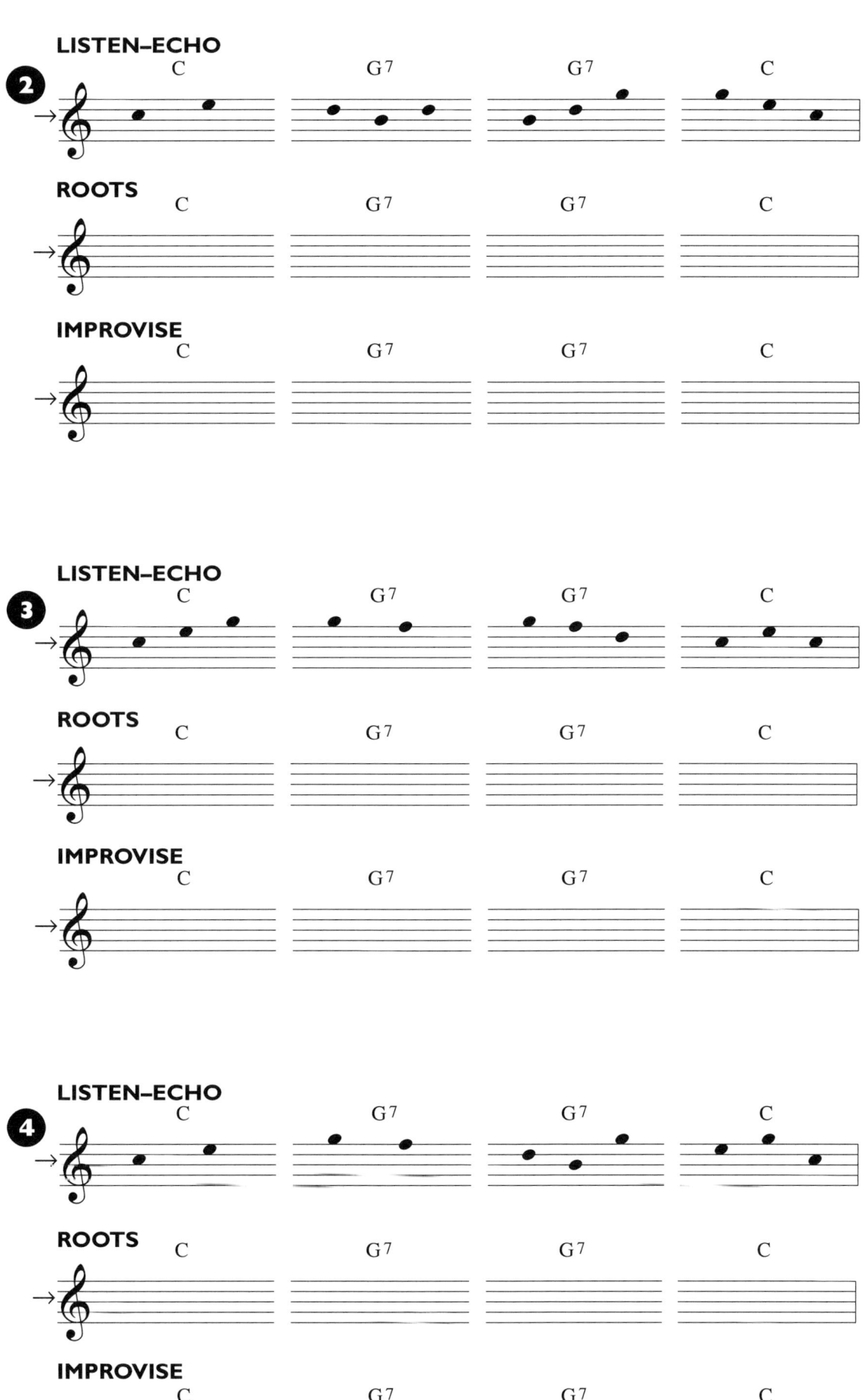

PART 3 – IMPROVISING MELODIC PHRASES

Sing improvised melodies to familiar repertoire.

Mary Ann
CD 1
Track 37

1. Listen to CD 1, Track 37. The performer sings the first phrase of "Mary Ann"; instead of continuing with the original second phrase, you hear an improvised melody that continues the harmonic progression. Listen to all four first phrases (antecedent phrases) and improvised second phrases (consequent phrases).

Example:

Mary Ann

Mary Ann
CD 1
Track 38

2. Listen to CD 1, Track 38. After hearing the first phrase (antecedent phrase) of "Mary Ann," continue the harmonic progression of the tune and sing a second phrase (consequent phrase) that is different from the original melody. Continue in a similar manner with the remaining phrases. Direct your melody toward chord tones, e.g., "DO," "MI," "SO" (CD 1, Track 38).

3. Perform in a similar manner on your instrument (CD 1, Track 38).

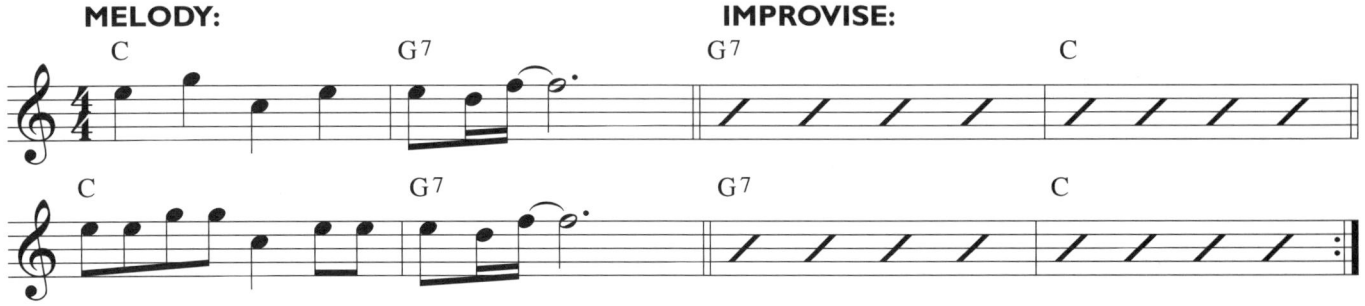

Mary Ann
CD 1
Track 48

4. Improvise both antecedent and consequent phrases to the harmonic progression of the tune (CD 1, Track 48). (The accompaniment repeats four times.)

PART 4 – LEARNING TO IMPROVISE
TONALLY   RHYTHMICALLY   EXPRESSIVELY

SEVEN SKILLS

Before you begin the Seven Skills, review "Mary Ann" (CD 1, Tracks 25–28).

1. SING and play the melody.

2. SING and PLAY the bass line (roots).

**Mary Ann
CD 1
Tracks 25–28,
39**

Skill 1

1. Listen to CD 1, Track 39. The performer improvises rhythm patterns to the bass line of "Mary Ann."

Example:

Mary Ann

Improvise Rhythms
on Chord Roots

2. Improvise rhythm patterns to the bass line of "Mary Ann." SING your improvisation, and then PLAY it on your instrument (CD 1, Track 48).

**Mary Ann
CD 1
Track 48**

Skill 2

1. Establish tonality in C major and SING each of the four parts on the next page for the harmonic functions of "Mary Ann." For example, SING "DO, SO, DO" – "DO, TI, DO" – "MI, FA, MI" – "SO, SO, SO."

2. Play each part on your instrument.

When in a group setting, each student should select a part to sing and play for Skills 3 and 4. When performing alone, start with the bass line (chord roots – Skill 1). Be sure to perform Skills 3 and 4 using the other three parts as well.

Example of Tonic and Dominant Harmony in C Major – 4 Parts:

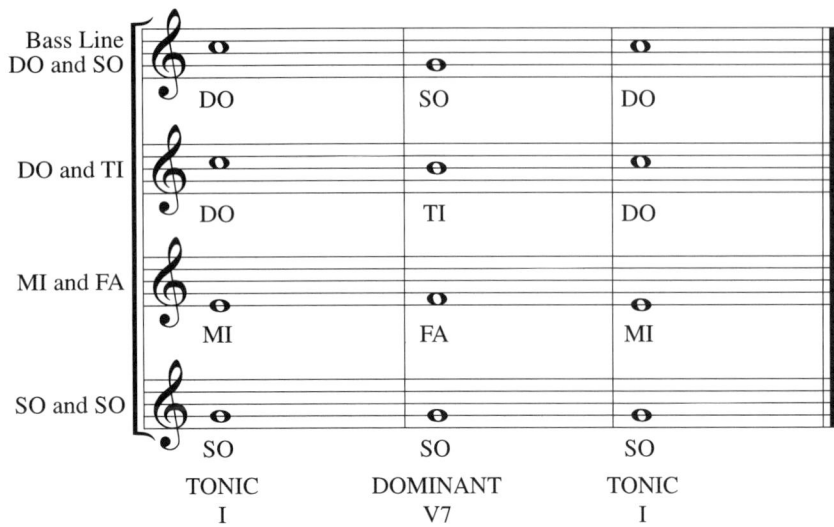

Skill 3

Mary Ann
CD 1
Tracks 47–48

Learn the harmonic rhythm for "Mary Ann" using the pitches from the harmony in **Skill 2**. SING every part. PLAY these parts on your instrument (CD 1, Tracks 47 and 48).

Skill 4

Using a neutral syllable (e.g., "doo"), improvise rhythm patterns to the harmonic progression using pitches learned in **Skill 2** (#2, 3, 4, and 5 below and on the facing page). Select a part and improvise rhythm patterns. Do this with each part. Interact with the melody (#1) and other parts (CD 1, Tracks 47 and 48). First SING, then PLAY these parts on your instrument.

Mary Ann

MELODY

BASS LINE; IMPROVISE RHYTHM

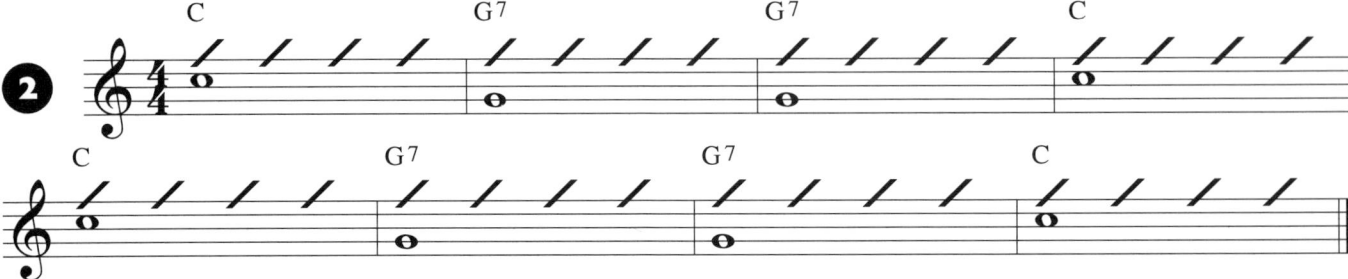

IMPROVISE RHYTHM ON "DO" AND "TI"

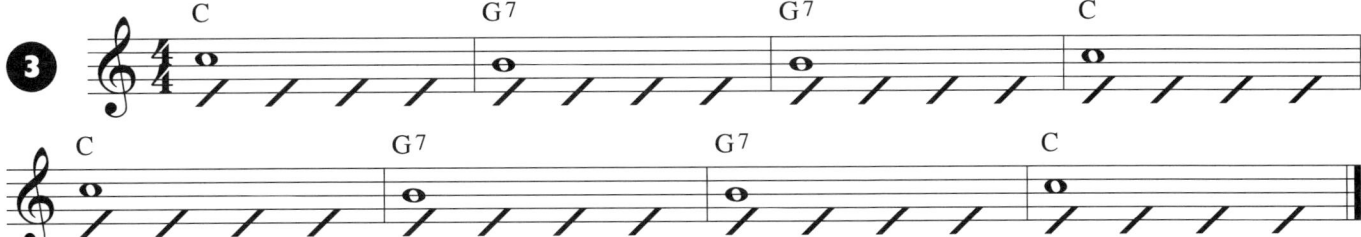

IMPROVISE RHYTHM ON "MI" AND "FA"

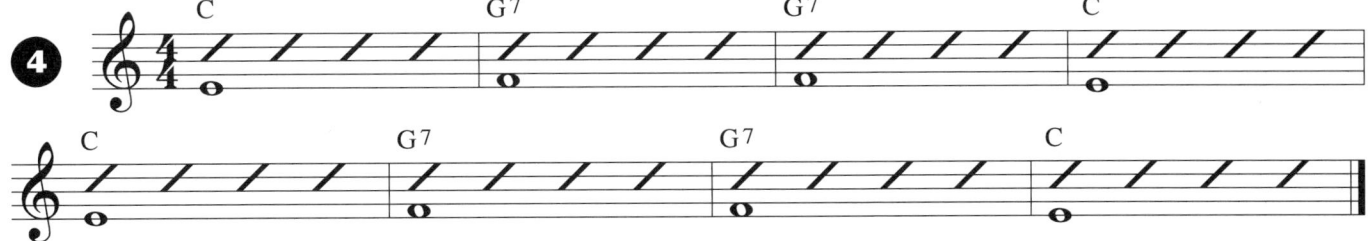

IMPROVISE RHYTHM ON "SO"

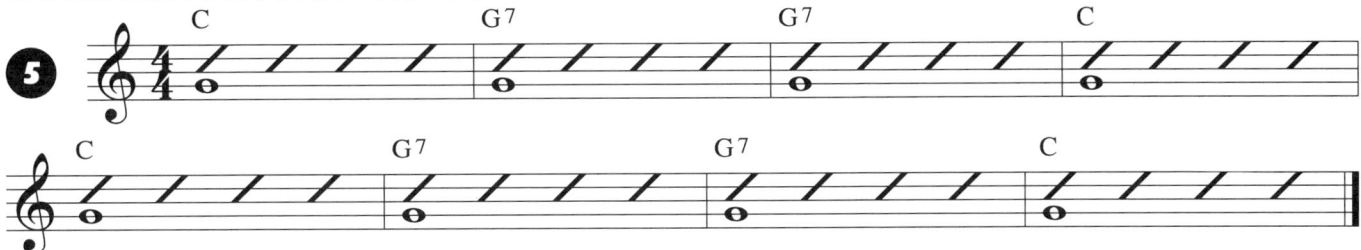

Skill 5

1. Listen to CD 1, Track 40. The performer improvises tonal patterns to the harmonic progression using macrobeats.

Mary Ann
CD 1
Track 40

Example:

Mary Ann
CD 1
Tracks 41, 48

2. Using macrobeats improvise (SING, then PLAY on your instrument) tonal patterns to the harmonic progression (CD 1, Track 48).

Skill 6

1. Listen to CD 1, Track 41. The performer improvises tonal patterns and rhythm patterns to the harmonic progression.

Example:

Mary Ann
CD 1
Tracks 42, 48

2. Improvise (SING, then PLAY on your instrument) tonal patterns and rhythm patterns to the harmonic progression (CD 1, Track 48).

Skill 7

1. Listen to CD 1, Track 42. The performer improvises by decorating and embellishing the melodic material in **Skill 6**.

Example:

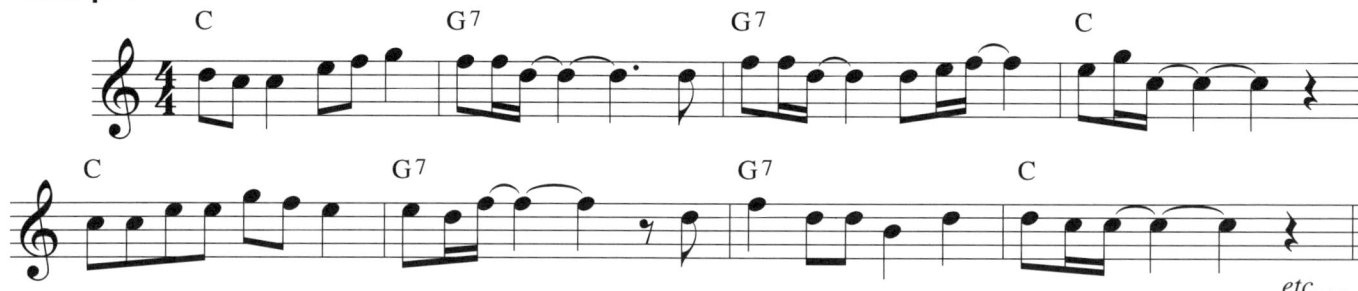

etc. . .

2. Decorate and embellish the melodic material in **Skill 6**. Improvise melodies to the harmonic progression (CD 1, Track 48). Learn to SING and PLAY the solos provided (CD 1, Tracks 43, 44, 45, and 46).

IMPROVISE to "Mary Ann" (CD 1, Tracks 47 and 48).

Mary Ann
CD 1
Tracks 43–48

PART 5 – READING AND WRITING

Rhythm Writing

1. Write the patterns on page 18 or notate improvised patterns. Establish meter and remember to group the notes into patterns and phrases before writing them.

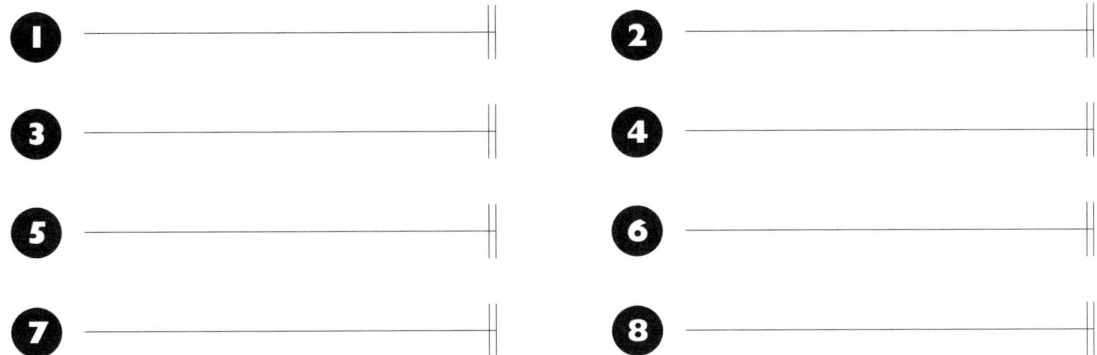

2. Write the series of patterns on page 19 or notate an improvised series of patterns.

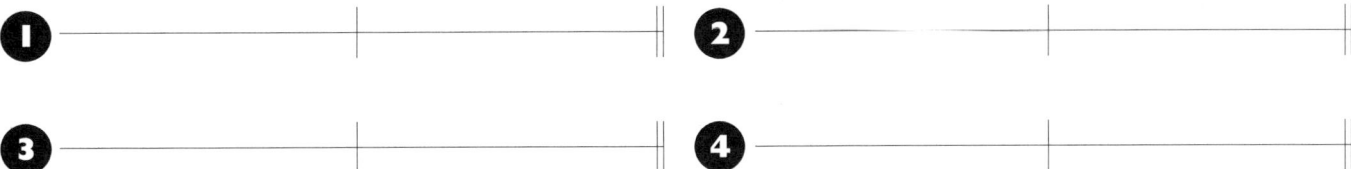

Tonal Writing

1. Write the patterns on page 20 or notate improvised patterns. Establish tonality and remember to group the notes into patterns and phrases before writing them.

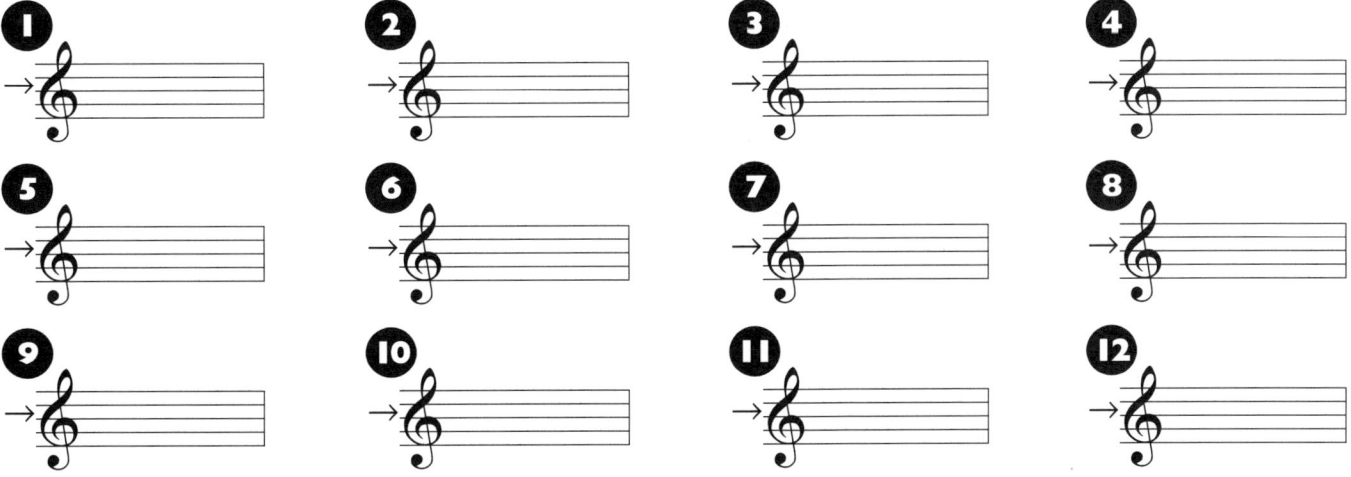

2. Write the series of patterns on page 22–23 or notate an improvised series of patterns for the progression.

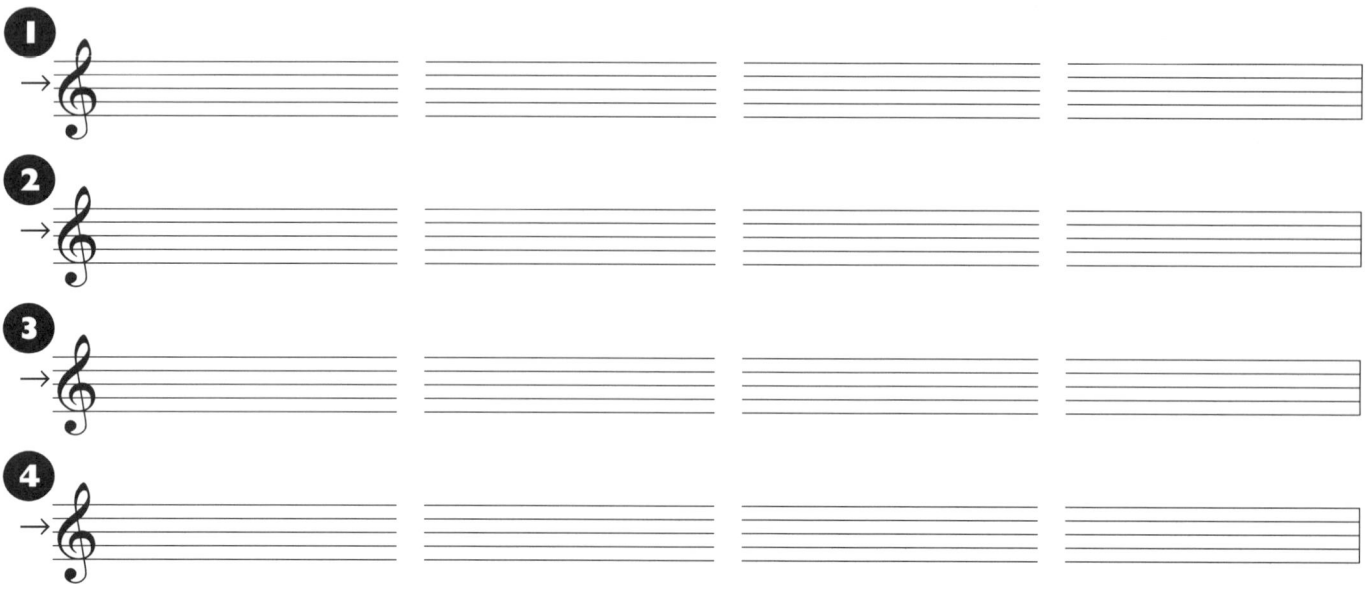

IMPROVISE – READ – COMPOSE

READ "Mary Ann" and IMPROVISE to the harmonic progression (CD 1, Tracks 47 and 48). SING and PLAY the melody and/or bass line on your instrument. Also, COMPOSE other melodies using the harmonic progression indicated and the tonal and rhythm vocabulary that you have learned.

Mary Ann

MELODY

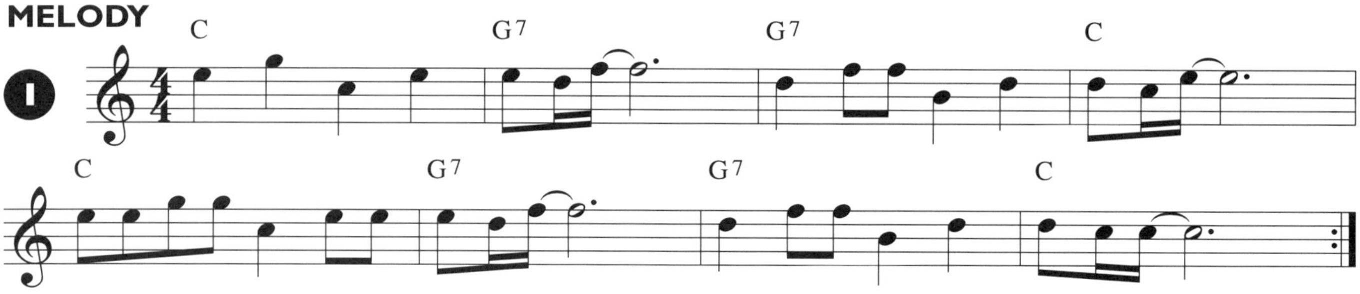

BASS LINE

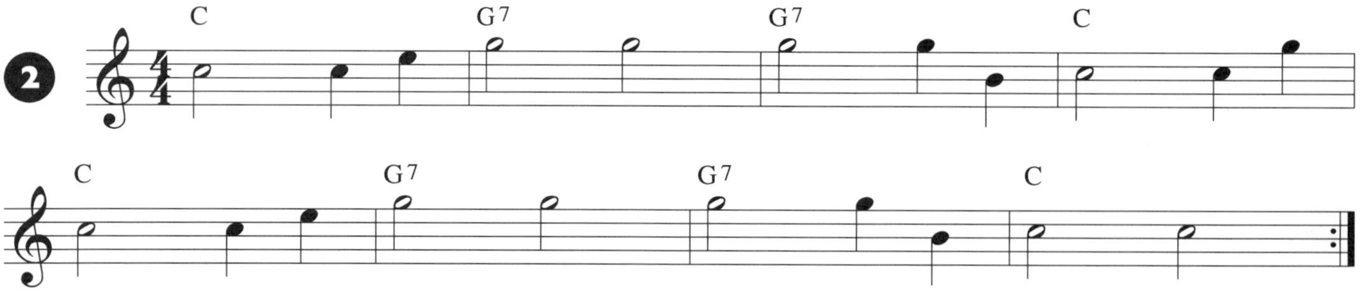

IMPROVISE

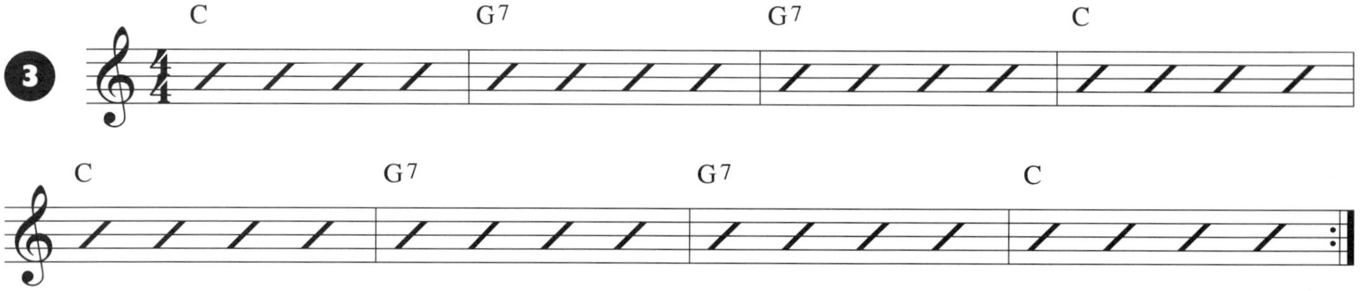

COMPOSE

4

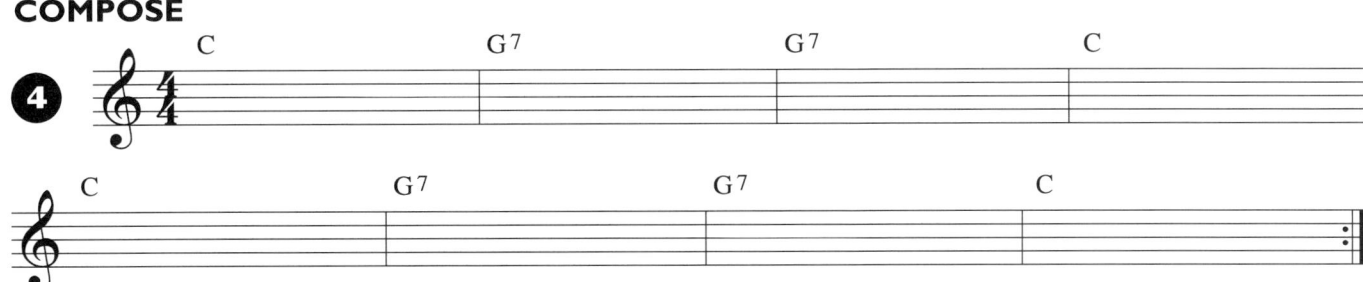

PART 6 – LEARNING SOLOS

Listen to CD 1, Tracks 43–46. The performer plays an interpretation of the melody followed by an improvised solo. Learn to sing and play the solo performed on the CD. Use the space provided to finish transcribing the solo on CD 1, Track 43, or to notate other solos. Analyze the solos for vocabulary and ideas to incorporate into your own improvised solos. See page v for suggestions about developing meaningful improvisations. Perform with the accompaniment on CD 1, Track 47 or 48.

Mary Ann
CD 1
Tracks 43–48

Mary Ann

PART I – REPERTOIRE

When first learning "Joshua," cover the notation.

1. LISTEN to "Joshua" – melody (CD 1, Track 49) and bass line (CD 1, Track 50).

2. With the accompaniment (CD 1, Track 51) SING the melody by ear with words and on a syllable such as "doo" and SING the bass line by ear on "doo."

3. PLAY your instrument by ear on the clicks immediately following each melodic pattern (CD 1, Track 52).

4. With the accompaniment (CD 1, Track 51) PLAY the melody and bass line on your instrument with the appropriate style of articulation. Personalize the tune using expressive phrasing, dynamics, and tonal and rhythmic variation.

Joshua
CD I
Tracks 49–52

Joshua

Traditional Spiritual

PART 2 – PATTERNS AND PROGRESSIONS

RHYTHM PATTERNS AND SERIES OF PATTERNS IN DUPLE METER (Swing Style)

Learn the patterns by ear – echo the patterns performed on the CD or by your teacher. When first learning the patterns, **cover the notation**.

Echo Rhythm Patterns for "Joshua"

Joshua
CD 1
Tracks 53–54

Learning these patterns is similar to learning words in a language. Becoming familiar with these patterns will improve your vocabulary for improvising rhythms to this tune.

1. ECHO the duple patterns on the syllable "bah" – CD 1, Track 53.

2. ECHO the patterns with rhythm syllables – CD 1, Track 54. The rhythm syllables will help you to organize and remember the patterns.

3. ECHO the patterns on your instrument on D–LA. Use the style(s) of articulation appropriate for "Joshua." CD 1, Track 53 or 54.

The number (2) tells how many macrobeats (DU) are in a measure. The symbol (♩) indicates what kind of note is a macrobeat (DU).
(♩=DU; ♪ ♪=DU DE; ♫♫=DU DI DE DI)

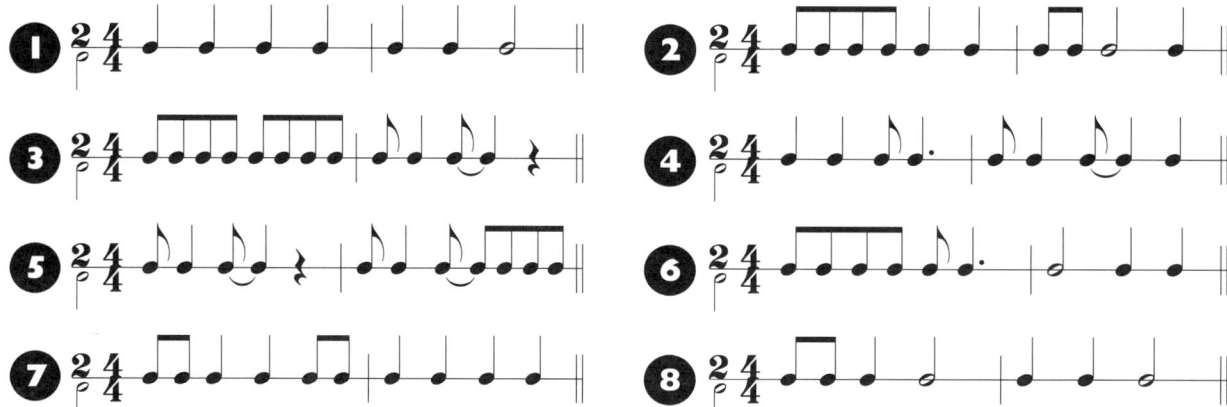

REPEAT AS NECESSARY

Improvise Rhythm Patterns for "Joshua"

Now that you are familiar with the rhythm patterns on CD 1, Tracks 53 and 54, improvise patterns using the rhythm vocabulary that you have learned.

Joshua
CD I
Tracks 53–54

1. Listen to the rhythm patterns performed on CD 1, Track 53. After each pattern IMPROVISE a different pattern using the syllable "bah."

2. Listen to the rhythm patterns performed on CD 1, Track 54. After each pattern IMPROVISE a different pattern using rhythm syllables.

3. IMPROVISE patterns on your instrument on D–LA. Use the style(s) of articulation appropriate for "Joshua." CD 1, Track 53 or 54.

Example:

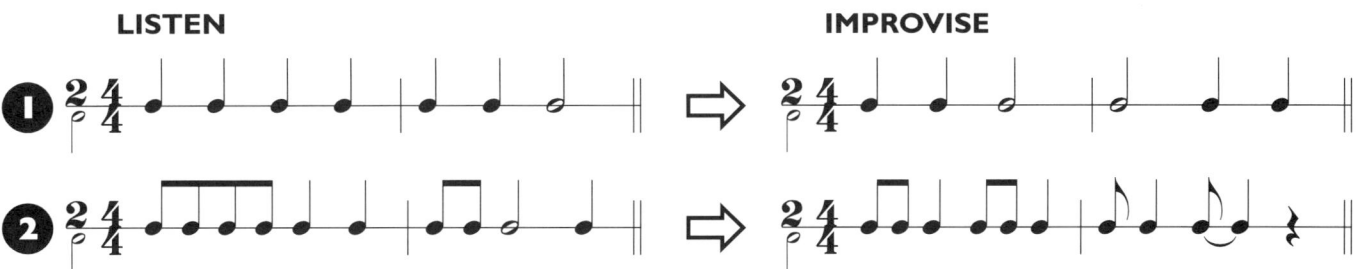

Continue with rhythm patterns 3 through 8 (CD 1, Tracks 53–54).

Echo and Improvise Series of Rhythm Patterns in Duple Meter

Improvising a series of patterns is like speaking a sentence or phrase in language.

Joshua
CD I
Tracks 55–56

1. ECHO rhythm phrases using the syllable "bah" (CD 1, Track 55), with rhythm syllables (CD 1, Track 56), and with your instrument on D–LA (CD 1, Track 55 or 56).

2. After each rhythm phrase, IMPROVISE a different phrase, using the syllable "bah" (CD 1, Track 55), with rhythm syllables (CD 1, Track 56), and with your instrument (CD 1, Track 55 or 56).

The number (2) tells how many macrobeats (DU) are in a measure. The symbol (♩) indicates what kind of note is a macrobeat (DU). (♩=DU; ♩ ♩=DU DE; ♫♫=DU DI DE DI)

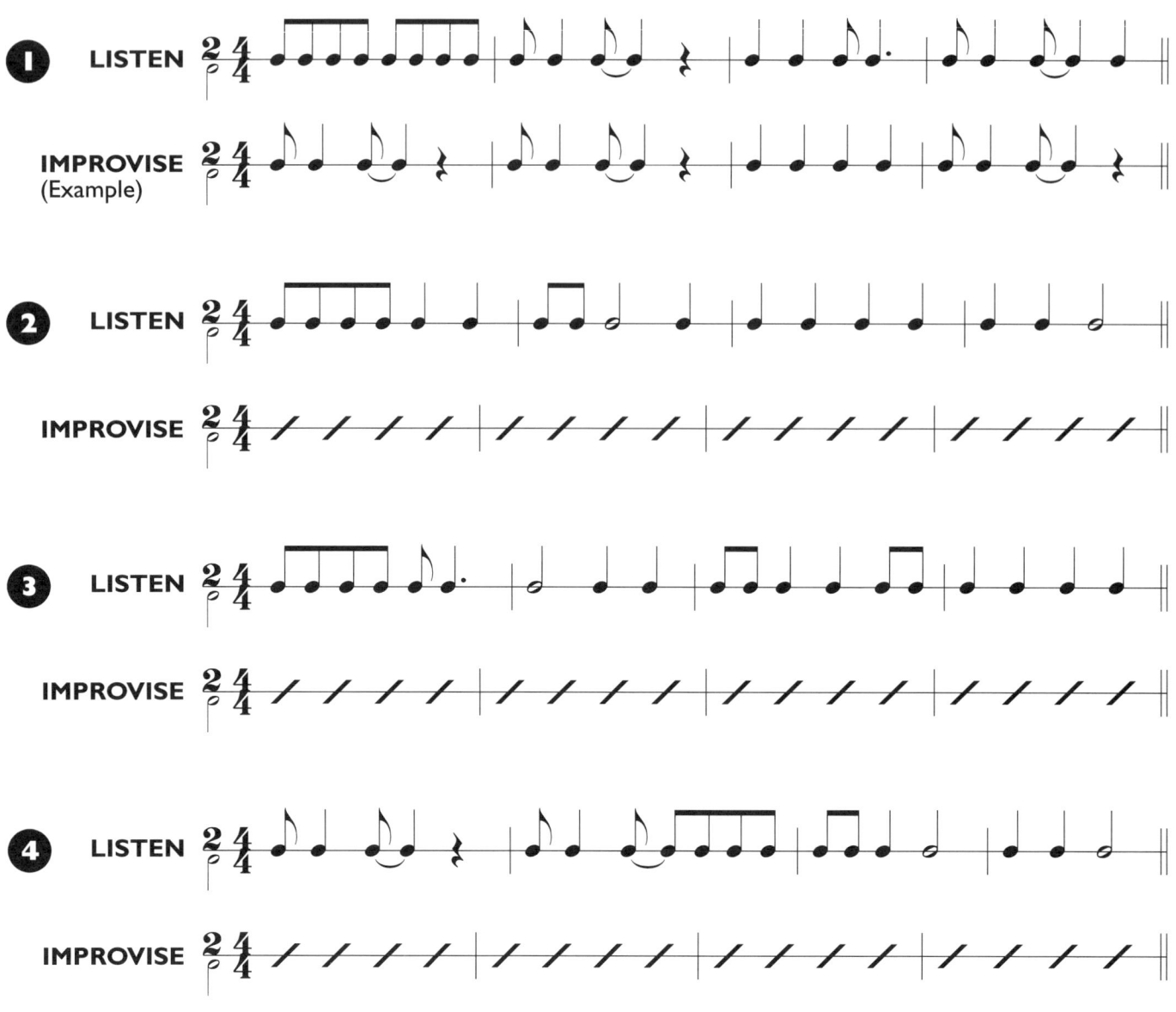

TONAL PATTERNS AND HARMONIC PROGRESSIONS

You have just learned to improvise rhythm patterns and phrases of rhythm patterns. Now learn to improvise tonal patterns and harmonic progressions. Improve your tonal vocabulary by learning the following tonal patterns, first with a neutral syllable and then with solfège.

Learn the patterns by ear – echo the patterns performed on the CD or by your teacher. When first learning the patterns, **cover the notation**.

Echo Tonal Patterns for "Joshua"

(D Minor – Tonic and Dominant)

1. ECHO, singing the following patterns on the syllable "bum" (CD 1, Track 57).

2. ECHO, singing the following patterns with solfège (CD 1, Track 58).

3. ECHO, playing each of the following patterns on your instrument (CD 1, Track 57 or 58).

Establish Tonality (Concert Pitch)

Joshua
CD 1
Tracks 57–58

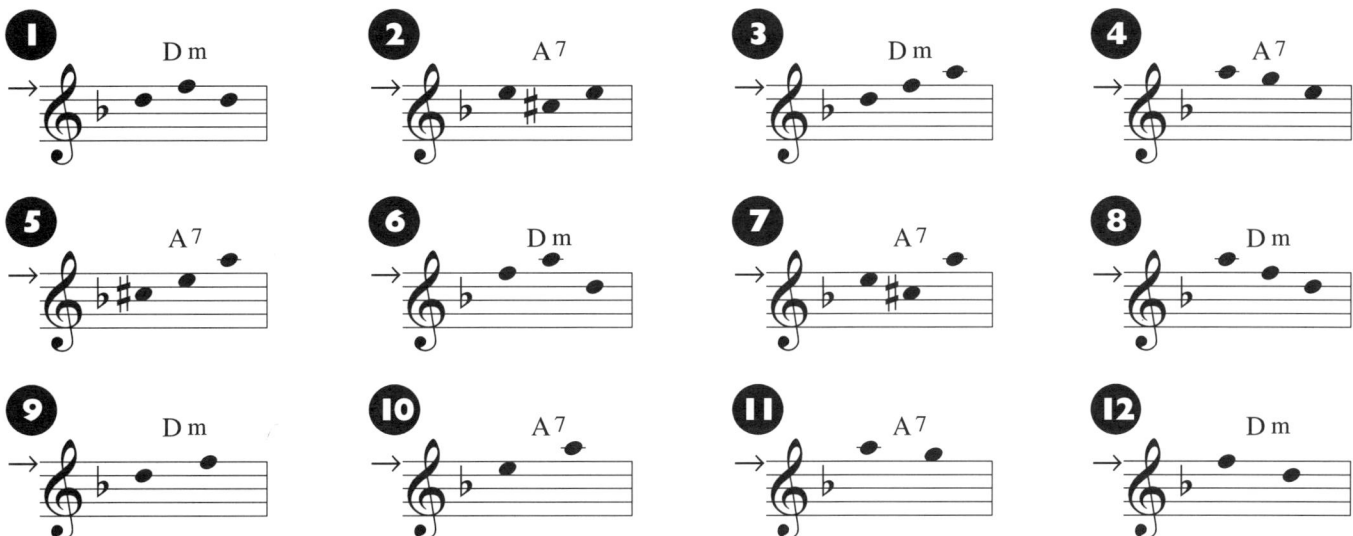

REPEAT AS NECESSARY

SING the Root (LA or MI) and NAME the Function (Tonic or Dominant) in D Minor.

1. LISTEN to the tonal patterns performed on CD 1, Track 58. After each pattern, SING the root of that function using tonal syllables, and immediately identify the harmonic function. SING: "LA" and "Tonic," or "MI" and "Dominant." (Dm=Tonic; A7=Dominant)

2. LISTEN again to CD 1, Track 58, and PLAY the roots on your instrument.

Joshua
CD 1
Track 58

Dm indicates TONIC function and A7 indicates DOMINANT function. A TONIC pattern in minor tonality includes any combination of "LA DO MI" and a DOMINANT pattern includes any combination of "MI RE TI SI."

SOLFÈGE SHOULD ALWAYS BE SUNG–NOT SPOKEN

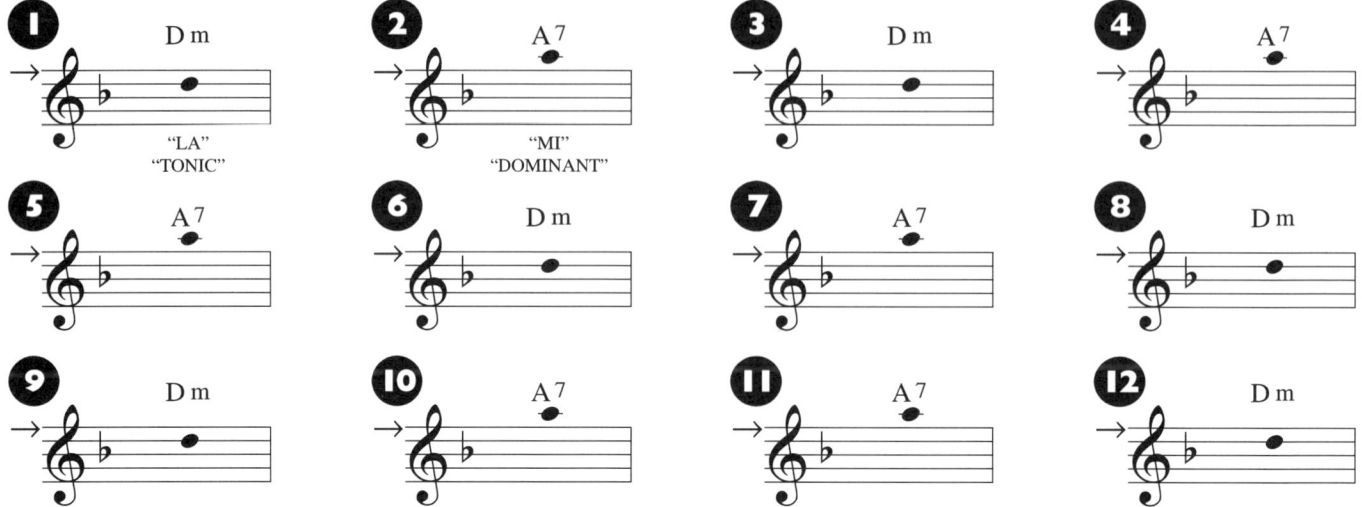

REPEAT AS NECESSARY

Improvise Tonal Patterns for "Joshua" (Tonic and Dominant Functions in D Minor)

Joshua
CD 1
Tracks 57–58

1. LISTEN again to the tonal patterns performed on CD 1, Tracks 57 and 58.

2. After each pattern, IMPROVISE a different pattern with the same harmonic function with a neutral syllable ("bum" – CD 1, Track 57).

3. After each pattern, IMPROVISE a different pattern with the same harmonic function with solfège (CD 1, Track 58).

4. After each pattern, IMPROVISE a different pattern with the same harmonic function on your instrument (CD 1, Track 57 or 58).

Example:

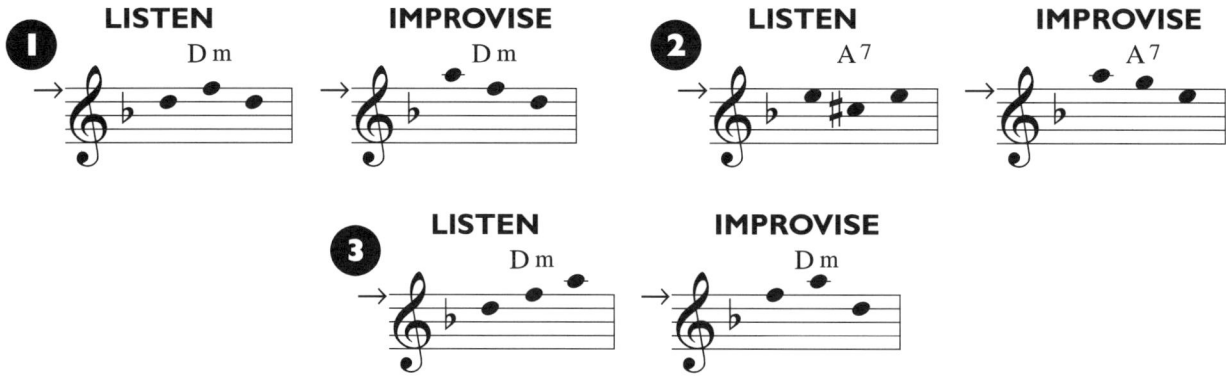

Continue with tonal patterns 4 through 12 (CD 1, Tracks 57–58).

ECHO and IMPROVISE Series of Tonic and Dominant Patterns in D Minor

Improvising a series of patterns to make a harmonic progression in music is like speaking a sentence or phrase in language. **Anticipate** and **predict** the harmonic progression. Where does the harmony go and where might it go?

1. Using the syllable "bum," ECHO (SING) the series of patterns (CD 1, Track 59).

2. Using solfège, ECHO (SING) the series of patterns (CD 1, Track 60).

3. ECHO the series of patterns on your instrument (CD 1, Track 59 or 60).

4. After each series of patterns, SING the bass line (roots) using solfège (CD 1, Track 60).

5. After each series of patterns, PLAY the bass line (roots) on your instrument (CD 1, Track 59 or 60).

6. After each series of patterns, IMPROVISE a different series of patterns over the same harmonic progression using solfège (CD 1, Track 60), with a neutral syllable ("bum" – CD 1, Track 59), and on your instrument (CD 1, Track 59 or 60).

Joshua
CD 1
Tracks 59–60

Example:

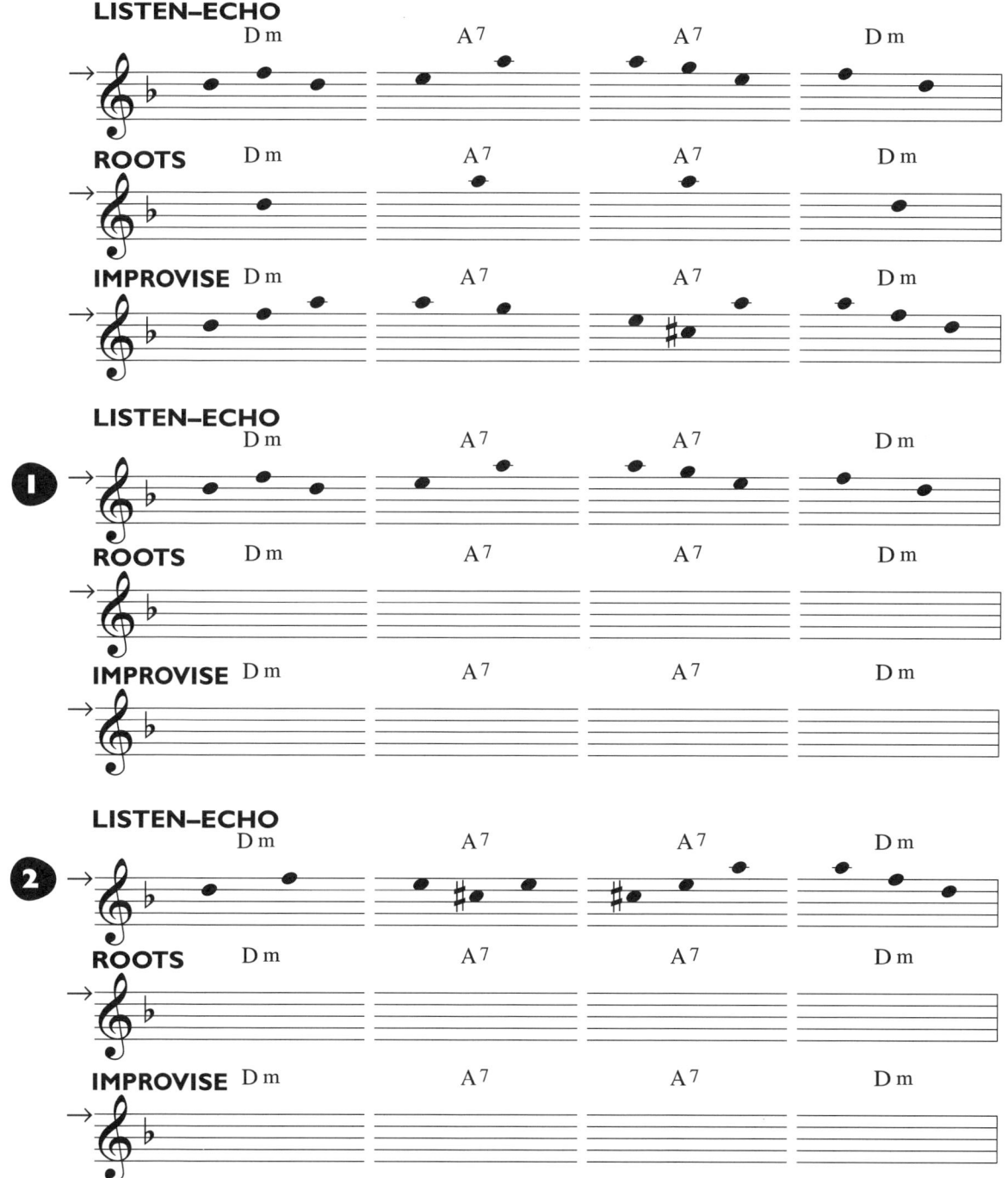

39

PART 3 – IMPROVISING MELODIC PHRASES

Sing improvised melodies to familiar repertoire.

Joshua
CD 1
Track 61

1. Listen to CD 1, Track 61. The performer sings the first phrase of "Joshua"; instead of continuing with the original second phrase, you hear an improvised melody that continues the harmonic progression. Listen to all four first phrases (antecedent phrases) and improvised second phrases (consequent phrases).

Example:

Joshua

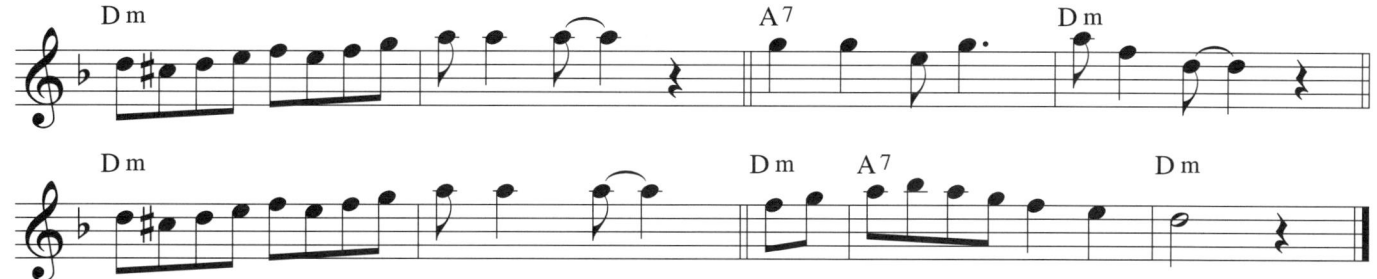

2. Listen to CD 1, Track 62. After hearing the first phrase (antecedent phrase) of "Joshua," continue the harmonic progression of the tune and sing a second phrase (consequent phrase) that is different from the original melody. Continue in a similar manner with the remaining phrases. Direct your melody toward chord tones, e.g., "LA," "DO," "MI" (CD 1, Track 62).

Joshua CD 1 Track 62

3. Perform in a similar manner on your instrument (CD 1, Track 62).

Now, you try:

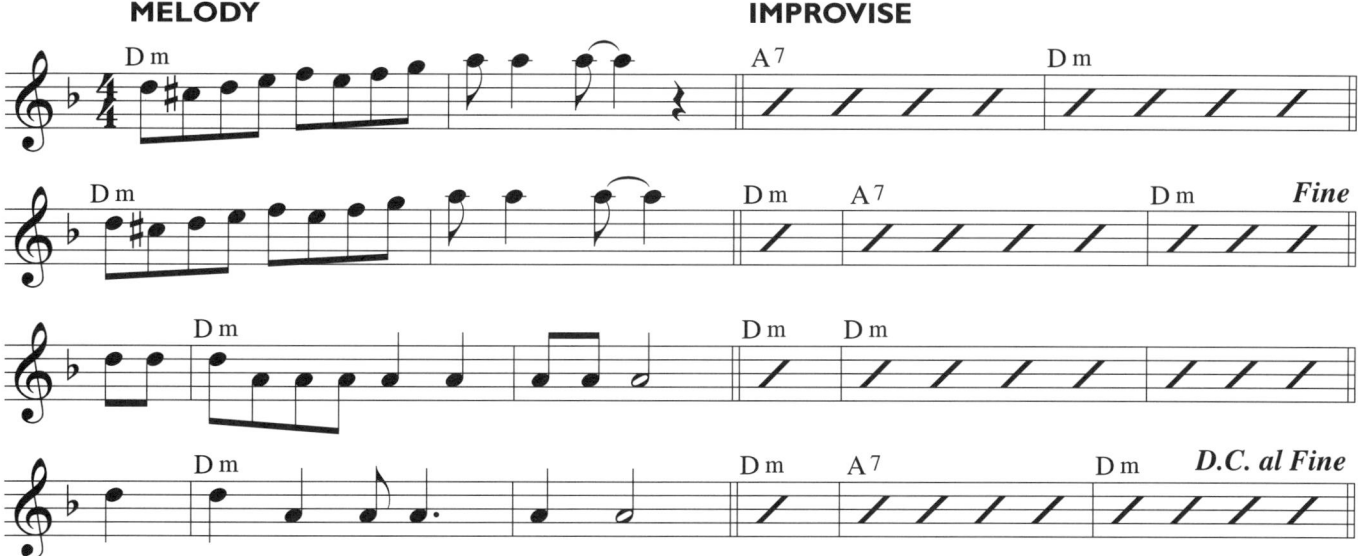

4. Improvise both antecedent and consequent phrases to the harmonic progression of the tune (CD 2, Track 5). (The accompaniment repeats three times.)

Joshua CD 2 Track 5

PART 4 – LEARNING TO IMPROVISE
TONALLY   RHYTHMICALLY   EXPRESSIVELY
SEVEN SKILLS

Joshua
CD 1
Tracks 49–52,
63

Before you begin the Seven Skills, review "Joshua" (CD 1, Tracks 49–52).

1. SING and PLAY the melody.

2. SING and PLAY the bass line (roots).

Skill 1

1. Listen to CD 1, Track 63. The performer improvises rhythm patterns to the bass line of "Joshua."

Example:

Joshua

Improvise Rhythms on Chord Roots

Joshua
CD 2
Track 5

2. Improvise rhythm patterns to the bass line of "Joshua." SING your improvisation with the neutral syllable "doo," and then PLAY it on your instrument (CD 2, Track 5).

Skill 2

1. Establish tonality in D minor and SING each of the four parts on the next page for the harmonic functions of "Joshua." For example, SING "LA, MI, LA" – "LA, SI, LA" – "DO, RE, DO" – "MI, MI, MI."

2. Play each part on your instrument.

When in a group setting, each student should select a part to sing and play for Skills 3 and 4. When performing alone, start with the bass line (chord roots – Skill 1). Be sure to perform Skills 3 and 4 using the other three parts as well.

Example of Tonic and Dominant Harmony in D Minor – 4 Parts:

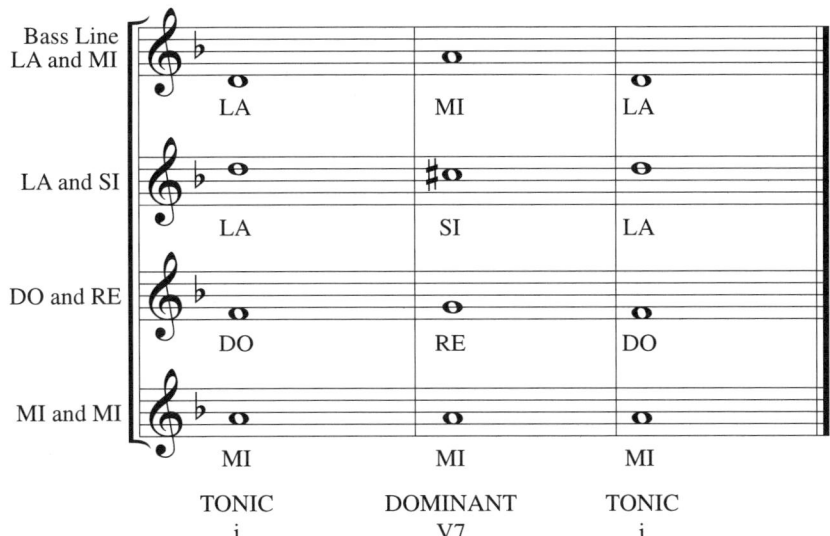

Skill 3

Learn the harmonic rhythm for "Joshua" using the pitches from the harmony in **Skill 2**. SING every part. PLAY these parts on your instrument (CD 2, Track 5).

Skill 4

Using a neutral syllable (e.g., "doo"), improvise rhythm patterns to the harmonic progression using pitches learned in **Skill 2** (#2, 3, 4, and 5 below and on the next page). Select a part and improvise rhythm patterns. Do this with each part. Interact with the melody (#1) and other parts (CD 2, Track 5). First SING, then PLAY these parts on your instrument.

Joshua
CD 2
Track 5

Joshua

MELODY

BASS LINE; IMPROVISE RHYTHM

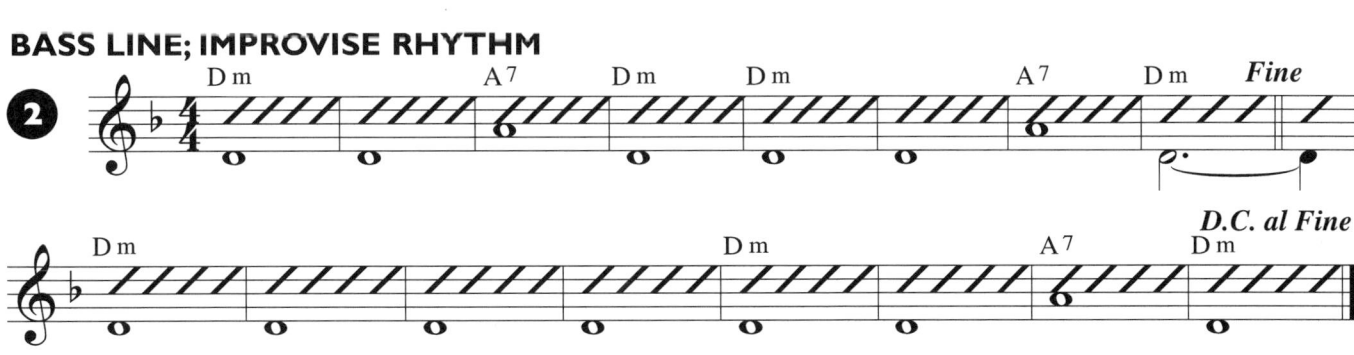

IMPROVISE RHYTHM ON "LA" AND "SI"

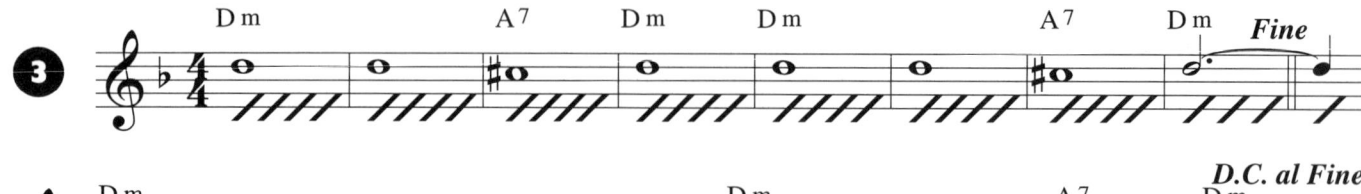

IMPROVISE RHYTHM ON "DO" AND "RE"

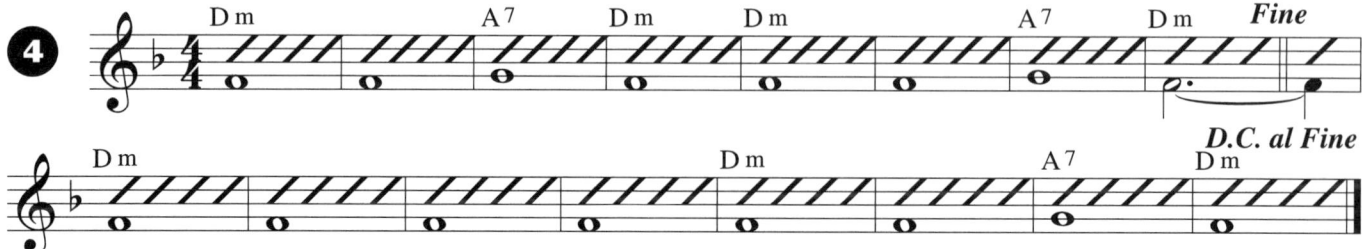

IMPROVISE RHYTHM ON "MI"

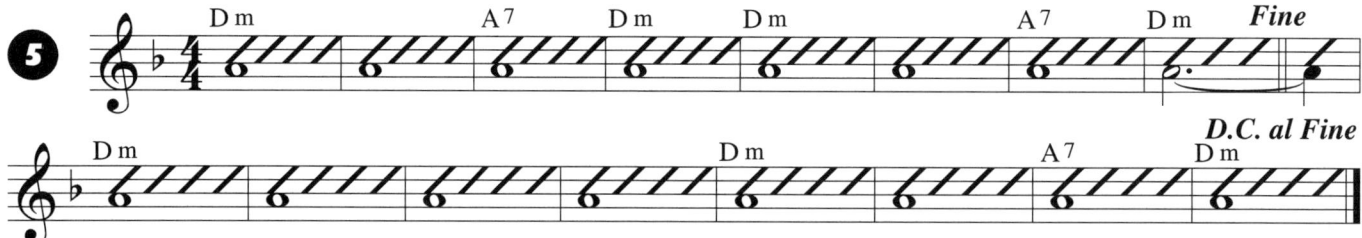

Skill 5

Joshua
CD 1
Track 64

1. Listen to CD 1, Track 64. The performer improvises tonal patterns to the harmonic progression using macrobeats.

Example:

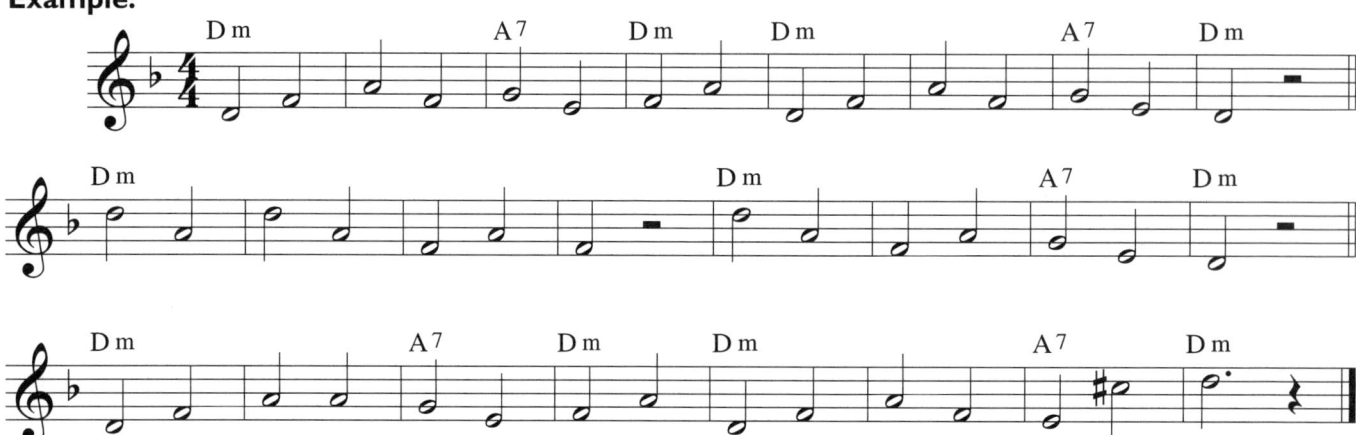

2. Using macrobeats improvise (SING, then PLAY on your instrument) tonal patterns to the harmonic progression (CD 2, Track 5).

Joshua
CD I
Track 65

CD 2
Track 5

Skill 6

I. Listen to CD 1, Track 65. The performer improvises tonal patterns and rhythm patterns to the harmonic progression.

Example:

2. Improvise (SING, then PLAY on your instrument) tonal patterns and rhythm patterns to the harmonic progression (CD 2, Track 5).

Joshua
CD I
Track 66

CD 2
Track 5

Skill 7

I. Listen to CD 1, Track 66. The performer improvises by decorating and embellishing the melodic material in **Skill 6**.

Example:

2. Decorate and embellish the melodic material in **Skill 6**. Improvise melodies to the harmonic progression (CD 2, Track 5). Learn to SING and PLAY the solos provided (CD 2, Tracks 1, 2, 3, and 4).

IMPROVISE to "Joshua" (CD 2, Track 5).

Joshua
CD 2
Tracks 1–5

PART 5 – READING AND WRITING

Rhythm Writing

I. Write the patterns on page 34 or notate improvised patterns. Establish meter and remember to group the notes into patterns and phrases before writing them.

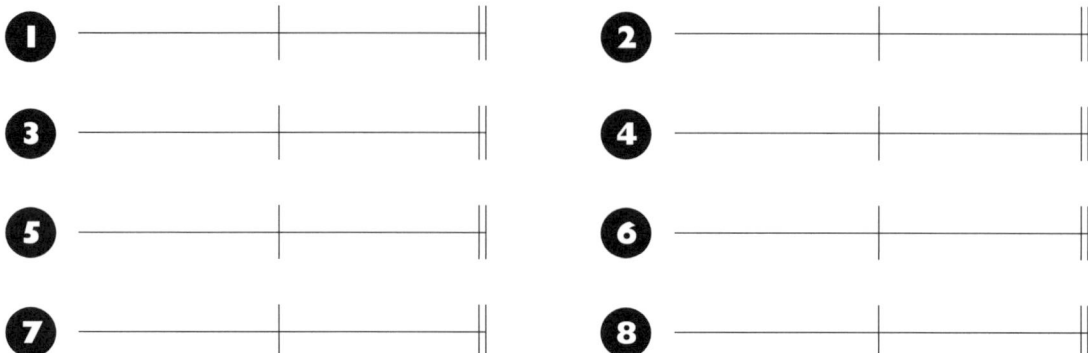

2. Write the series of patterns on page 36 or notate an improvised series of patterns.

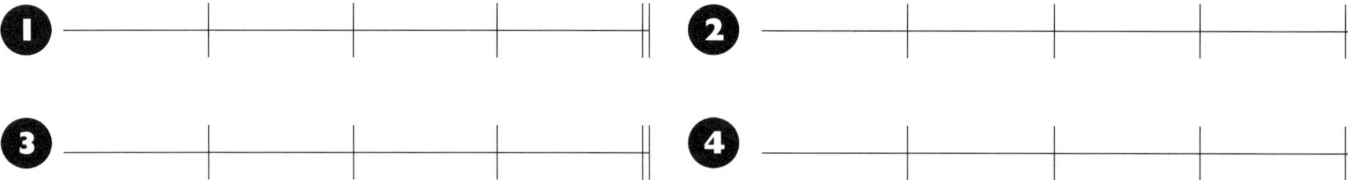

Tonal Writing

I. Write the patterns on page 37 or notate improvised patterns. Establish tonality and remember to group the notes into patterns and phrases before writing them.

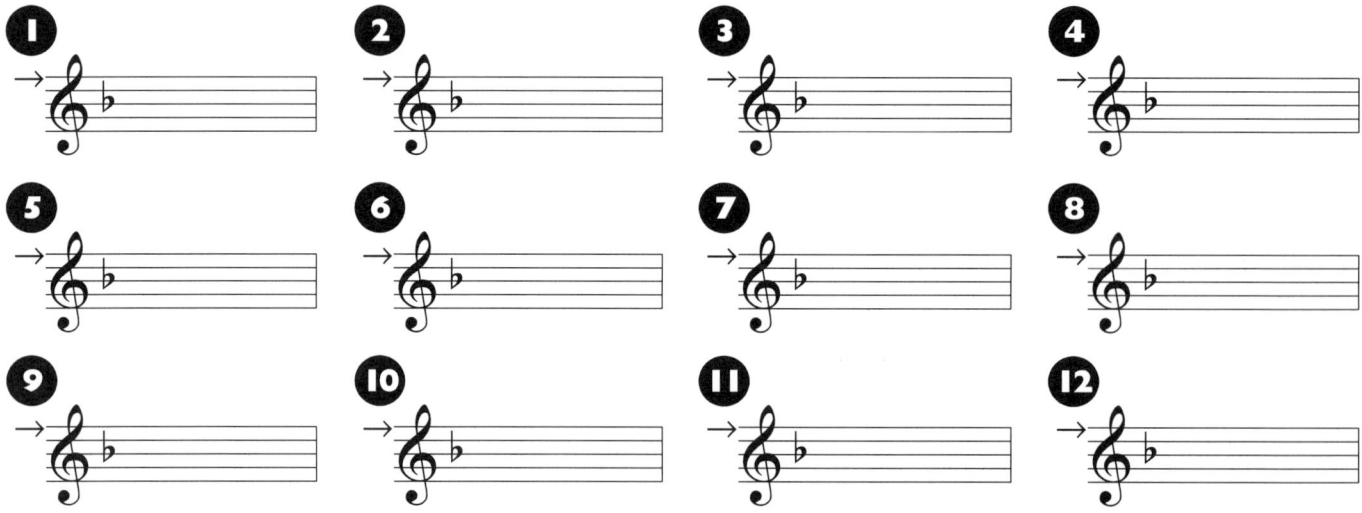

2. Write the series of patterns on pages 39–40 or notate an improvised series of patterns for the progression.

IMPROVISE – READ – COMPOSE

READ "Joshua" and IMPROVISE to the harmonic progression (CD 2, Track 5). SING and PLAY the melody and/or bass line on your instrument. Also, COMPOSE other melodies using the harmonic progression indicated and the tonal and rhythm vocabulary that you have learned.

Joshua

IMPROVISE

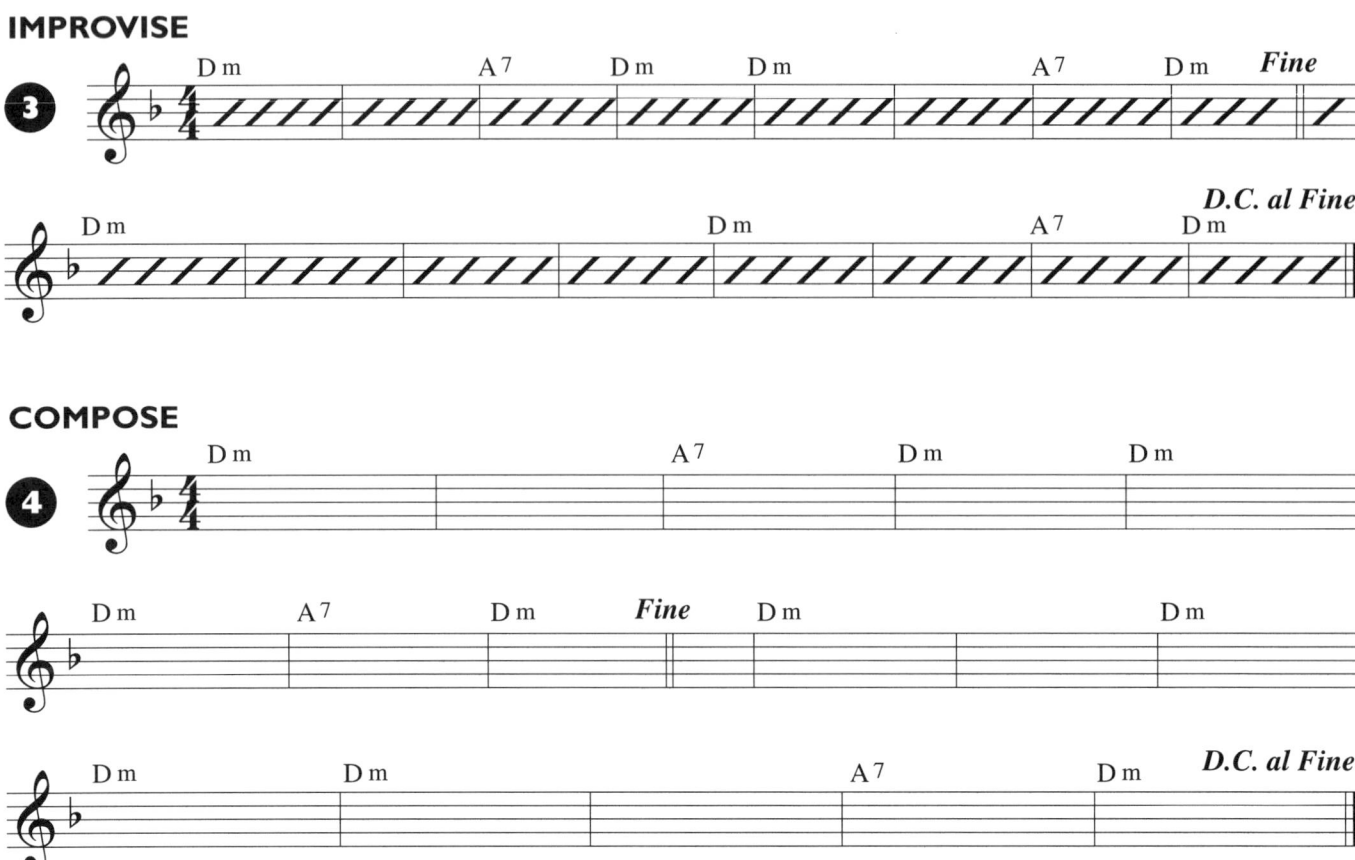

COMPOSE

PART 6 – LEARNING SOLOS

Joshua
CD 2
Tracks 1–5

Listen to CD 2, Tracks 1–4. The performer plays an interpretation of the melody followed by an improvised solo. Learn to sing and play the solo performed on the CD. Use the space provided to finish transcribing the solo on CD 2, Track 1, or to notate other solos. Analyze the solos for vocabulary and ideas to incorporate into your own improvised solos. See page v for suggestions about developing meaningful improvisations. Perform with the accompaniment on CD 2, Track 5.

Joshua

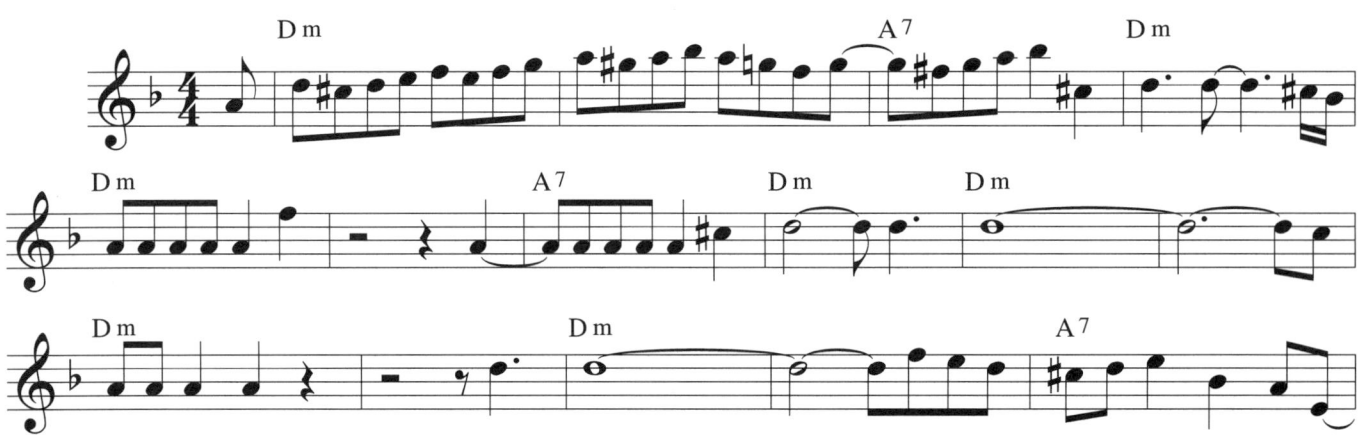

PART 1 – REPERTOIRE

When first learning "Simple Gifts," cover the notation.

1. LISTEN to "Simple Gifts" – melody (CD 2, Track 6) and bass line (CD 2, Track 7).

2. With the accompaniment (CD 2, Track 8) SING the melody by ear with words and on a syllable such as "doo" and SING the bass line by ear on "doo."

3. PLAY your instrument by ear on the clicks immediately following each melodic pattern (CD 2, Track 9).

4. With the accompaniment (CD 2, Track 8) PLAY the melody and bass line on your instrument with the appropriate style of articulation. Personalize the tune using expressive phrasing, dynamics, and tonal and rhythmic variation.

Simple Gifts CD 2 Tracks 6–9

Simple Gifts

Joseph Brackett, Jr.

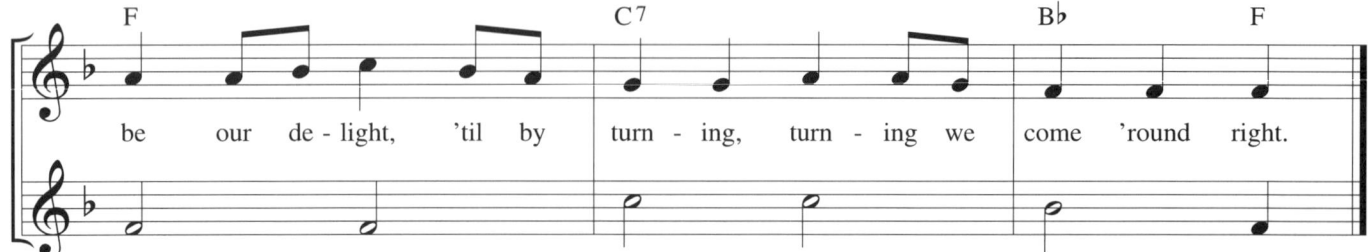

be our de‑light, 'til by turn‑ing, turn‑ing we come 'round right.

PART 2 – PATTERNS AND PROGRESSIONS

RHYTHM PATTERNS AND SERIES OF PATTERNS IN DUPLE METER

> Learn the patterns by ear – echo the patterns performed on the CD or by your teacher. When first learning the patterns, **cover the notation**.

Echo Rhythm Patterns for "Simple Gifts"

Simple Gifts
CD 2
Tracks 10–11

Learning these patterns is similar to learning words in a language. Becoming familiar with these patterns will improve your vocabulary for improvising rhythms to this tune.

1. ECHO the duple patterns on the syllable "bah" – CD 2, Track 10.

2. ECHO the patterns with rhythm syllables – CD 2, Track 11. The rhythm syllables will help you to organize and remember the patterns.

3. ECHO the patterns on your instrument on F–DO. Use the style(s) of articulation appropriate for "Simple Gifts." CD 2, Track 10 or 11.

The number (2) tells how many macrobeats (DU) are in a measure. The symbol (♩) indicates what kind of note is a macrobeat (DU). (♩=DU; ♪ ♪=DU DE; ♫♫=DU TA DE TA)

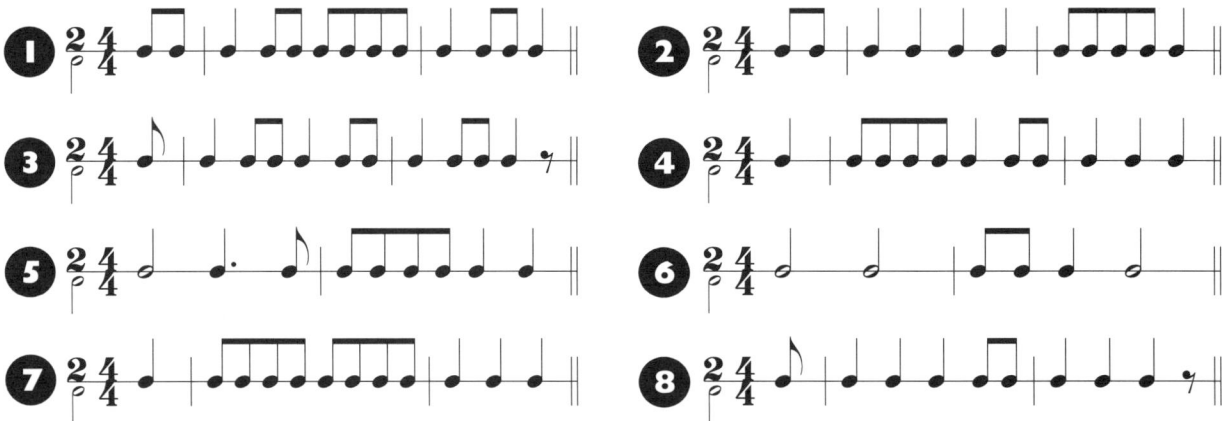

REPEAT AS NECESSARY

52

Improvise Rhythm Patterns for "Simple Gifts"

Now that you are familiar with the rhythm patterns on CD 2, Tracks 10 and 11, improvise patterns using the rhythm vocabulary that you have learned.

Simple Gifts
CD 2
Tracks 10–11

1. Listen to the rhythm patterns performed on CD 2, Track 10. After each pattern IMPROVISE a different pattern using the syllable "bah."

2. Listen to the rhythm patterns performed on CD 2, Track 11. After each pattern IMPROVISE a different pattern using rhythm syllables.

3. IMPROVISE patterns on your instrument on F–DO. Use the style(s) of articulation appropriate for "Simple Gifts." CD 2, Track 10 or 11.

Example:

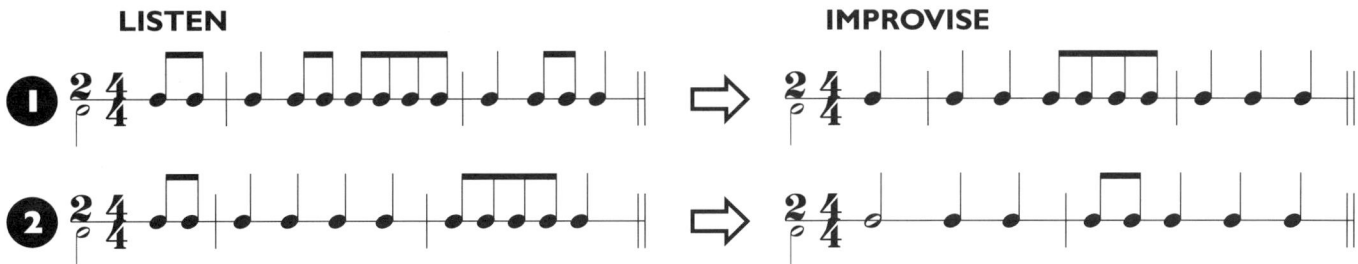

LISTEN   **IMPROVISE**

Continue with rhythm patterns 3 through 8 (CD 2, Tracks 10–11).

Echo and Improvise Series of Rhythm Patterns in Duple Meter

Improvising a series of patterns is like speaking a sentence or phrase in language.

Simple Gifts
CD 2
Tracks 12–13

1. ECHO rhythm phrases using the syllable "bah" (CD 2, Track 12), with rhythm syllables (CD 2, Track 13), and with your instrument on F–DO (CD 2, Track 12 or 13).

2. After each rhythm phrase, IMPROVISE a different phrase using the syllable "bah" (CD 2, Track 12), with rhythm syllables (CD 2, Track 13), and with your instrument (CD 2, Track 12 or 13).

The number (2) tells how many macrobeats (DU) are in a measure. The symbol (♩) indicates what kind of note is a macrobeat (DU). (♩ =DU; ♪ ♪ =DU DE; ♫♫ =DU TA DE TA)

REPEAT AS NECESSARY

TONAL PATTERNS AND HARMONIC PROGRESSIONS

You have just learned to improvise rhythm patterns and phrases of rhythm patterns. Now learn to improvise tonal patterns and harmonic progressions. Improve your tonal vocabulary by learning the following tonal patterns, first with a neutral syllable and then with solfège.

Learn the patterns by ear – echo the patterns performed on the CD or by your teacher. When first learning the patterns, **cover the notation**.

Echo Tonal Patterns for "Simple Gifts"

(F Major – Tonic and Dominant)

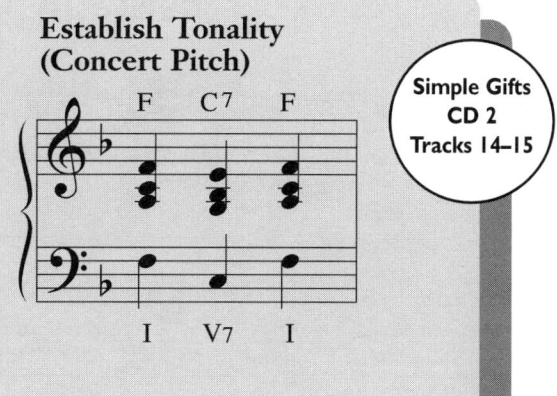

Establish Tonality (Concert Pitch)

Simple Gifts
CD 2
Tracks 14–15

1. ECHO, singing the following patterns on the syllable "bum" (CD 2, Track 14).

2. ECHO, singing the following patterns with solfège (CD 2, Track 15).

3. ECHO, playing each of the following patterns on your instrument (CD 2, Track 14 or 15).

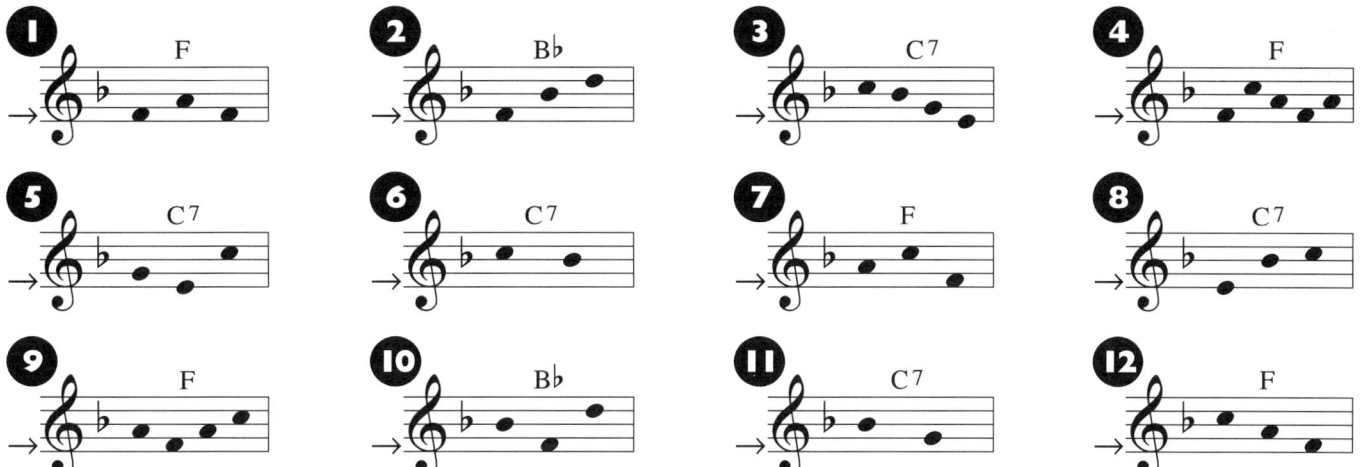

REPEAT AS NECESSARY

SING the Root (DO, FA, or SO) and NAME the Function (Tonic, Subdominant, or Dominant) in F Major.

1. LISTEN to the tonal patterns performed on CD 2, Track 15. After each pattern, SING the root of that function using tonal syllables, and immediately identify the harmonic function. SING: "DO" and "Tonic," "FA" and "Subdominant," or "SO" and "Dominant." (F=Tonic; Bb=Subdomninant; C7=Dominant)

Simple Gifts
CD 2
Track 15

2. LISTEN again to CD 2, Track 15, and PLAY the roots on your instrument.

F indicates TONIC function, Bb indicates SUBDOMINANT function, and C7 indicates DOMINANT function. A TONIC pattern in major tonality includes any combination of "DO MI SO"; a SUBDOMINANT pattern includes any combination of "FA LA DO"; and a DOMINANT pattern includes any combination of "SO FA RE TI."

SOLFÈGE SHOULD ALWAYS BE SUNG–NOT SPOKEN

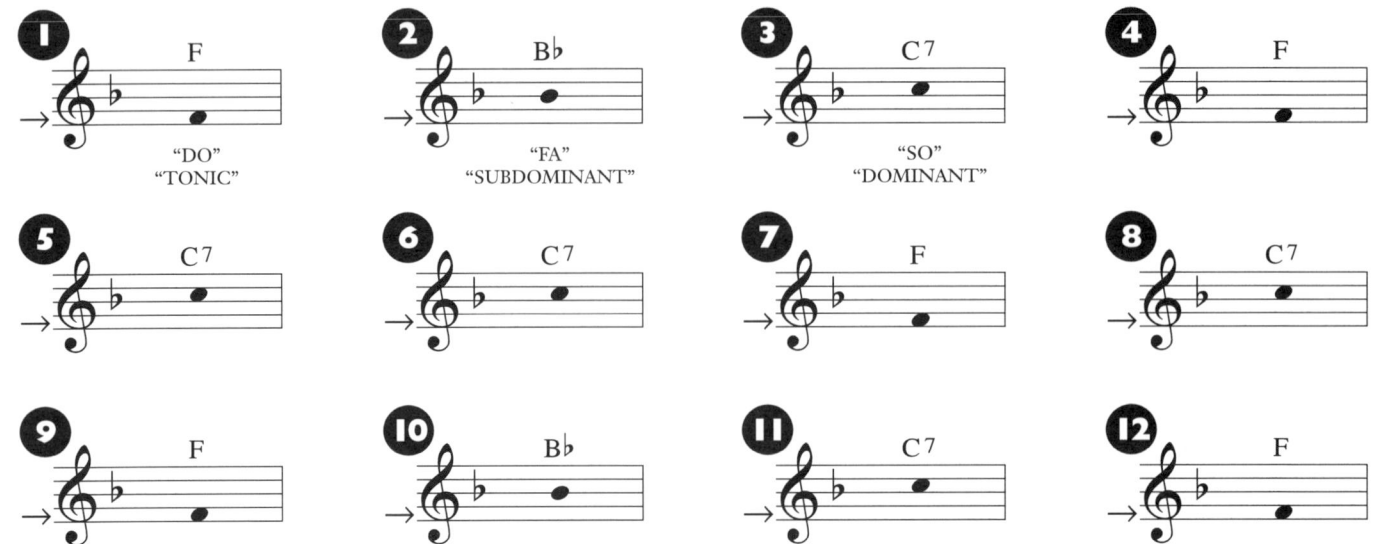

1 F — "DO" "TONIC"
2 B♭ — "FA" "SUBDOMINANT"
3 C7 — "SO" "DOMINANT"
4 F
5 C7
6 C7
7 F
8 C7
9 F
10 B♭
11 C7
12 F

REPEAT AS NECESSARY

Improvise Tonal Patterns for "Simple Gifts" (Tonic, Subdominant, and Dominant Functions in F Major)

Simple Gifts
CD 2
Tracks 14–15

1. LISTEN again to the tonal patterns performed on CD 2, Tracks 14 and 15.

2. After each pattern, IMPROVISE a different pattern with the same harmonic function with a neutral syllable ("bum" – CD 2, Track 14).

3. After each pattern, IMPROVISE a different pattern with the same harmonic function with solfège (CD 2, Track 15).

4. After each pattern, IMPROVISE a different pattern with the same harmonic function on your instrument (CD 2, Track 14 or 15).

Example:

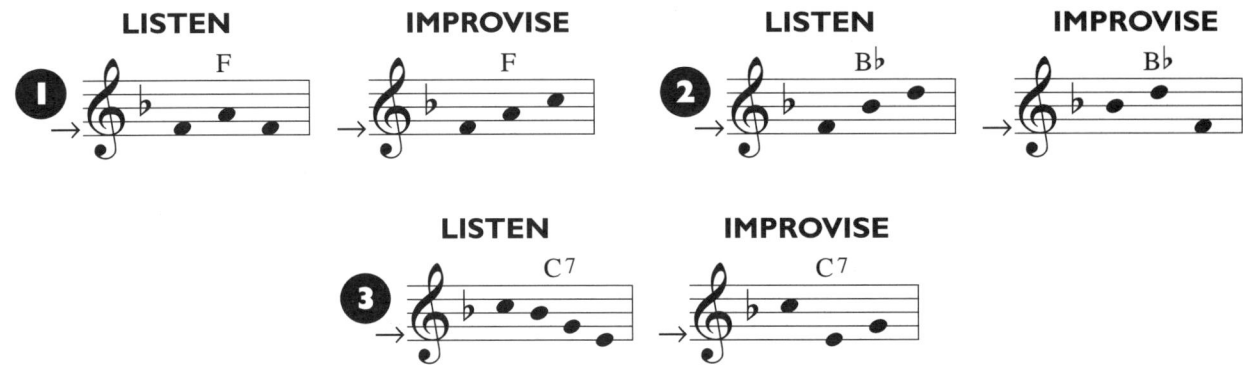

LISTEN — IMPROVISE   LISTEN — IMPROVISE   LISTEN — IMPROVISE

Continue with tonal patterns 4 through 12 (CD 2, Tracks 14–15).

ECHO and IMPROVISE Series of Tonic and Dominant Patterns in F Major

Improvising a series of patterns to make a harmonic progression in music is like speaking a sentence or phrase in language. **Anticipate** and **predict** the harmonic progression. Where does the harmony go and where might it go?

1. Using the syllable "bum," ECHO (SING) the series of patterns (CD 2, Track 16).

2. Using solfège, ECHO (SING) the series of patterns (CD 2, Track 17).

3. ECHO the series of patterns on your instrument (CD 2, Track 16 or 17).

4. After each series of patterns, SING the bass line (roots) using solfège (CD 2, Track 17).

5. After each series of patterns, PLAY the bass line (roots) on your instrument (CD 2, Track 16 or 17).

6. After each series of patterns, IMPROVISE a different series of patterns over the same harmonic progression using solfège (CD 2, Track 17), with a neutral syllable ("bum" – CD 2, Track 16), and on your instrument (CD 2, Track 16 or 17).

Simple Gifts
CD 2
Tracks 16–17

Example:

57

PART 3 – IMPROVISING MELODIC PHRASES

Sing improvised melodies to familiar repertoire.

Simple Gifts
CD 2
Track 18

1. Listen to CD 2, Track 18. The performer sings the first phrase of "Simple Gifts"; instead of continuing with the original second phrase, you hear an improvised melody that continues the harmonic progression. Listen to all four first phrases (antecedent phrases) and improvised second phrases (consequent phrases).

Example:

Simple Gifts

2. Listen to CD 2, Track 19. After hearing the first phrase (antecedent phrase) of "Simple Gifts," continue the harmonic progression of the tune and sing a second phrase (consequent phrase) that is different from the original melody. Continue in a similar manner with the remaining phrases. Direct your melody toward chord tones, e.g., "DO," "MI," "SO" (CD 2, Track 19).

Simple Gifts
CD 2
Track 19

3. Perform in a similar manner on your instrument (CD 2, Track 19).

Now, you try:

4. Improvise both antecedent and consequent phrases to the harmonic progression of the tune (CD 2, Track 26). (The accompaniment repeats two times.)

Simple Gifts
CD 2
Track 26

PART 4 – LEARNING TO IMPROVISE
TONALLY   RHYTHMICALLY   EXPRESSIVELY

SEVEN SKILLS

**Simple Gifts
CD 2
Tracks 6–9, 20**

Before you begin the Seven Skills, review "Simple Gifts" (CD 2, Tracks 6–9).

1. SING and PLAY the melody.

2. SING and PLAY the bass line (roots).

Skill 1

1. Listen to CD 2, Track 20. The performer improvises rhythm patterns to the bass line of "Simple Gifts."

Example:

Simple Gifts

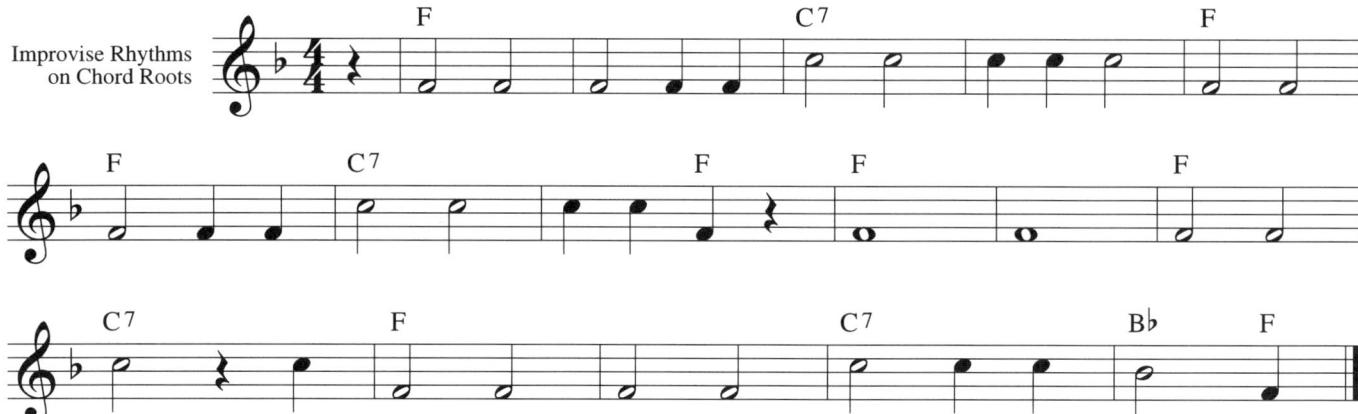

**Simple Gifts
CD 2
Track 26**

2. Improvise rhythm patterns to the bass line of "Simple Gifts." SING your improvisation with the neutral syllable "doo," and then PLAY it on your instrument (CD 2, Track 26).

Skill 2

1. Establish tonality in F major and SING each of the four parts on the next page for the harmonic functions of "Simple Gifts." For example, SING "DO, FA, SO, DO" – "DO, DO, TI, DO" – "MI, FA, FA, MI" – "SO, LA, SO, SO."

2. Play each part on your instrument.

When in a group setting, each student should select a part to sing and play for Skills 3 and 4. When performing alone, start with the bass line (chord roots – Skill 1). Be sure to perform Skills 3 and 4 using the other three parts as well.

Example of Tonic, Subdominant, and Dominant Harmony in F Major – 4 Parts:

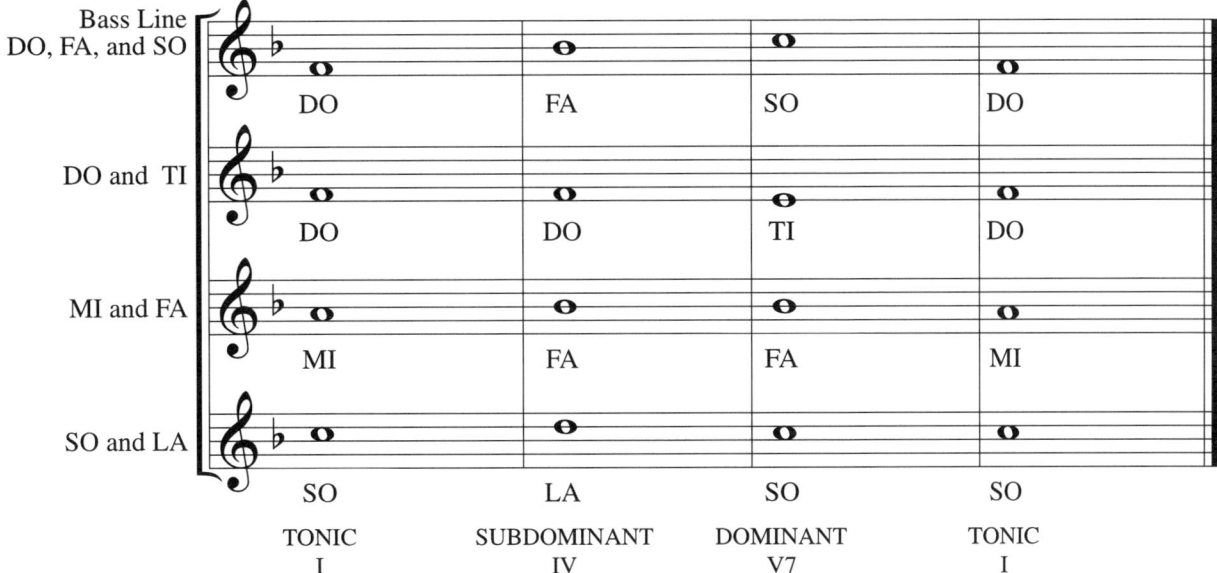

	TONIC I	SUBDOMINANT IV	DOMINANT V7	TONIC I
Bass Line DO, FA, and SO	DO	FA	SO	DO
DO and TI	DO	DO	TI	DO
MI and FA	MI	FA	FA	MI
SO and LA	SO	LA	SO	SO

Skill 3

Learn the harmonic rhythm for "Simple Gifts" using the pitches from the harmony in **Skill 2**. SING every part. PLAY these parts on your instrument (CD 2, Track 26).

Simple Gifts
CD 2
Track 26

Skill 4

Using a neutral syllable (e.g., "doo"), improvise rhythm patterns to the harmonic progression using pitches learned in **Skill 2** (#2, 3, 4, and 5 below and on the next page). Select a part and improvise rhythm patterns. Do this with each part. Interact with the melody (#1) and other parts (CD 2, Track 26). First SING, then PLAY these parts on your instrument.

Simple Gifts

MELODY

①

BASS LINE; IMPROVISE RHYTHM

②

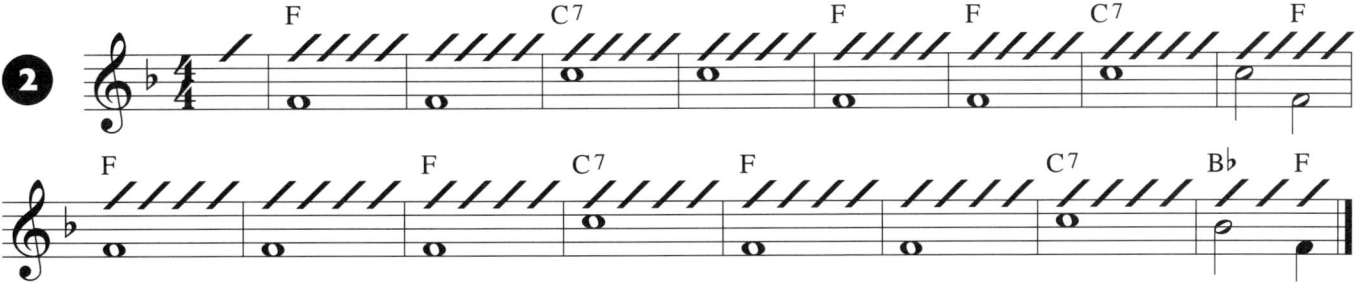

IMPROVISE RHYTHM ON "DO" AND "TI"

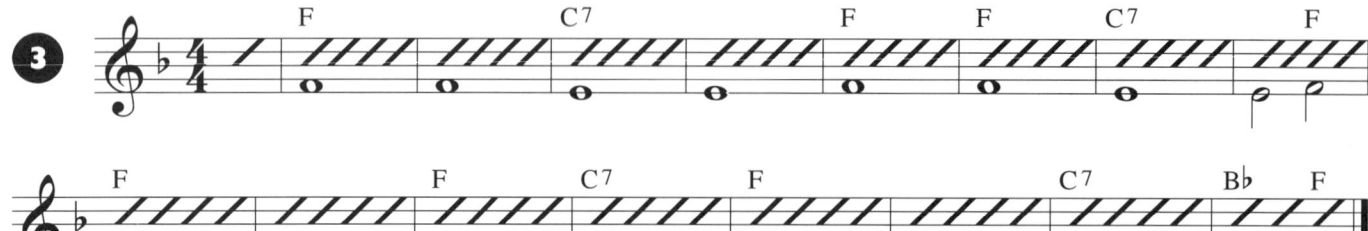

IMPROVISE RHYTHM ON "MI" AND "FA"

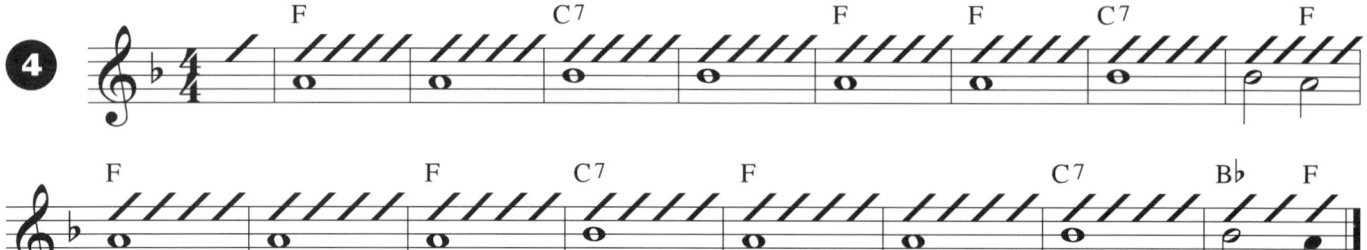

IMPROVISE RHYTHM ON "SO" AND "LA"

Skill 5

Simple Gifts
CD 2
Track 21

1. Listen to CD 2, Track 21. The performer improvises tonal patterns to the harmonic progression using macrobeats.

Example:

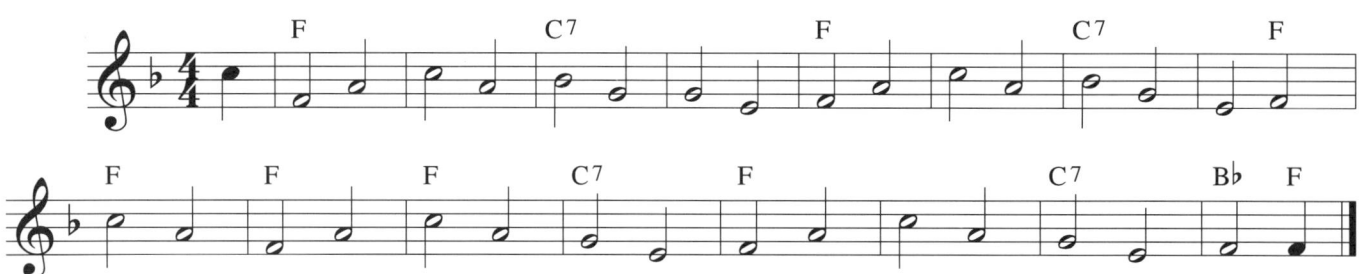

2. Using macrobeats improvise (SING, then PLAY on your instrument) tonal patterns to the harmonic progression (CD 2, Track 26).

Skill 6

1. Listen to CD 2, Track 22. The performer improvises tonal patterns and rhythm patterns to the harmonic progression.

Simple Gifts
CD 2
Tracks 22, 26

Example:

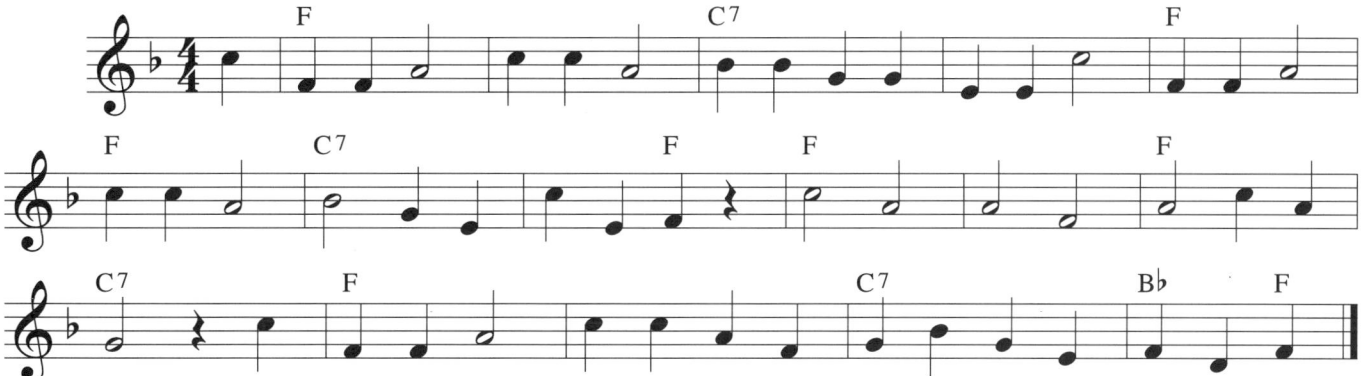

2. Improvise (SING, then PLAY on your instrument) tonal patterns and rhythm patterns to the harmonic progression (CD 2, Track 26).

Skill 7

1. Listen to CD 2, Track 23. The performer improvises by decorating and embellishing the melodic material in **Skill 6**.

Simple Gifts
CD 2
Tracks 23, 26

Example:

2. Decorate and embellish the melodic material in **Skill 6**. Improvise melodies to the harmonic progression (CD 2, Track 26). Learn to SING and PLAY the solos provided (CD 2, Tracks 24 and 25).

IMPROVISE to "Simple Gifts" (CD 2, Track 26).

Simple Gifts
CD 2
Tracks 24–26

PART 5 – READING AND WRITING

Rhythm Writing

1. Write the patterns on page 52 or notate improvised patterns. Establish meter and remember to group the notes into patterns and phrases before writing them.

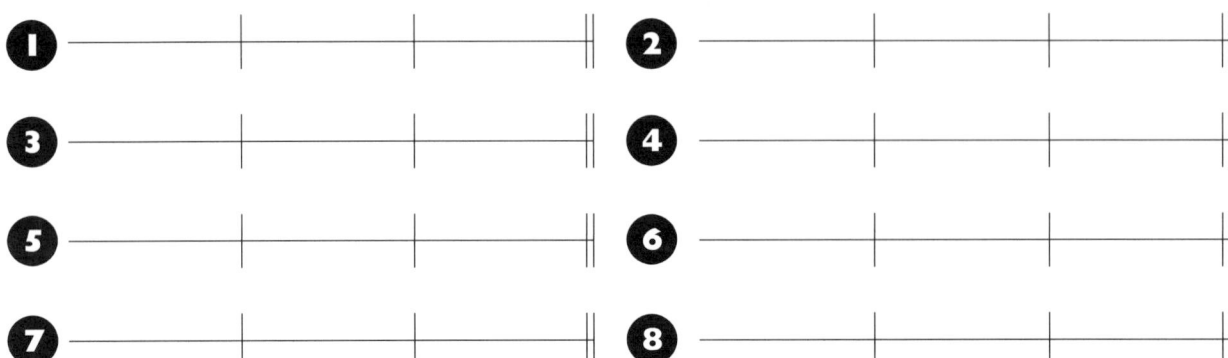

2. Write the series of patterns on page 54 or notate an improvised series of patterns.

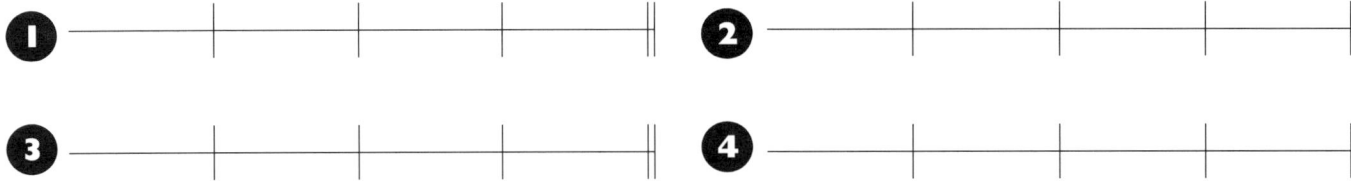

Tonal Writing

1. Write the patterns on page 55 or notate improvised patterns. Establish tonality and remember to group the notes into patterns and phrases before writing them.

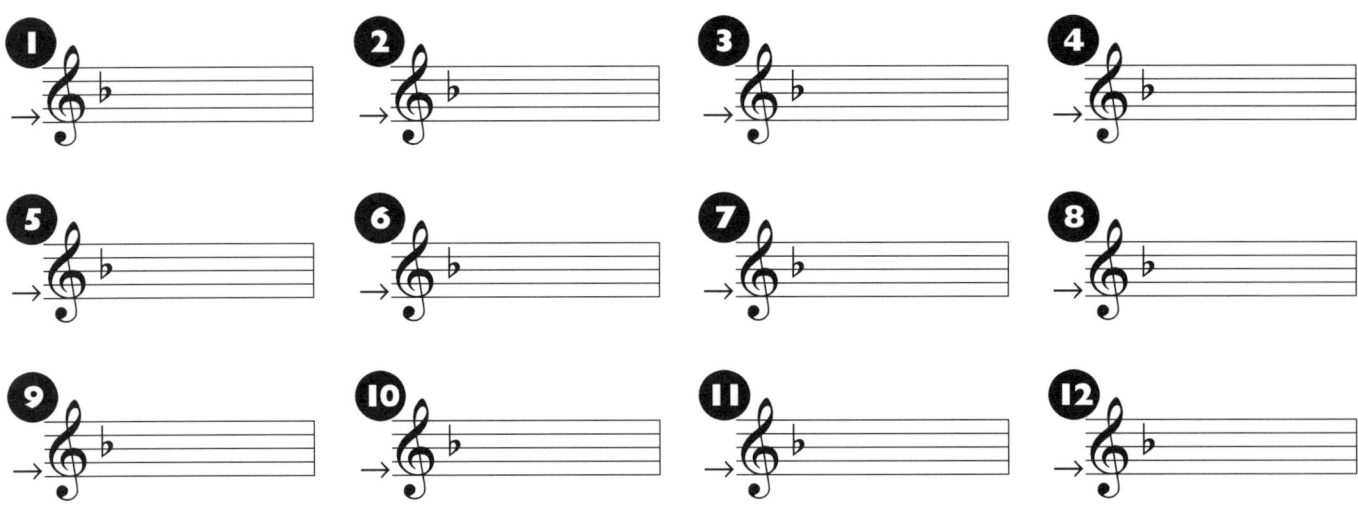

2. Write the series of patterns on pages 57–58 or notate an improvised series of patterns for the progression.

IMPROVISE – READ – COMPOSE

READ "Simple Gifts" and IMPROVISE to the harmonic progression (CD 2, Track 26). SING and PLAY the melody and/or bass line on your instrument. Also, COMPOSE other melodies using the harmonic progression indicated and the tonal and rhythm vocabulary that you have learned.

Simple Gifts

IMPROVISE

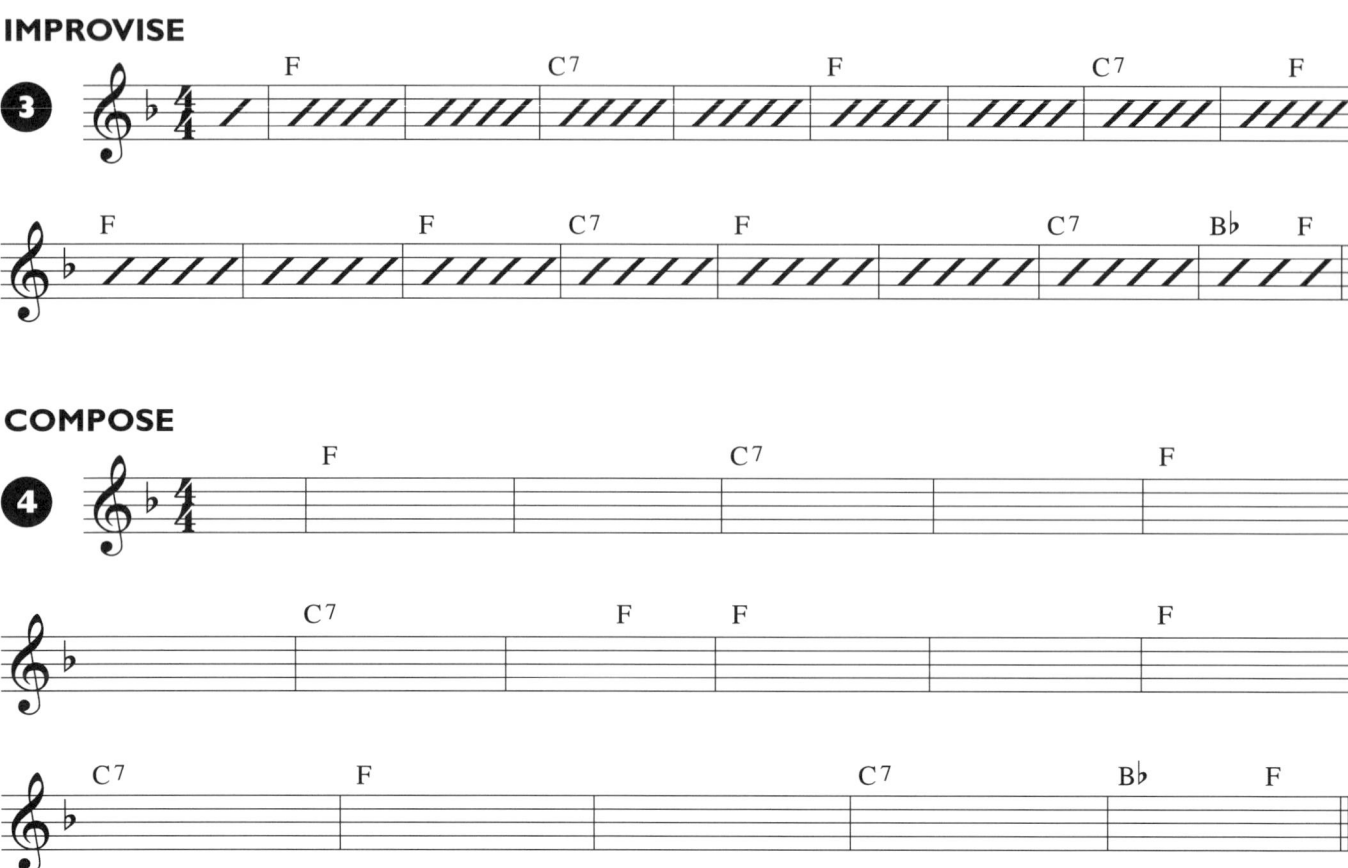

COMPOSE

PART 6 – LEARNING SOLOS

Listen to CD 2, Tracks 24 and 25. The performer plays an interpretation of the melody followed by an improvised solo. Learn to sing and play the solo performed on the CD. Use the space provided to finish transcribing the solo on CD 2, Track 25, or to notate other solos. Analyze the solos for vocabulary and ideas to incorporate into your own improvised solos. See page v for suggestions about developing meaningful improvisations. Perform with the accompaniment on CD 2, Track 26.

Simple Gifts
CD 2
Tracks 24–26

Simple Gifts

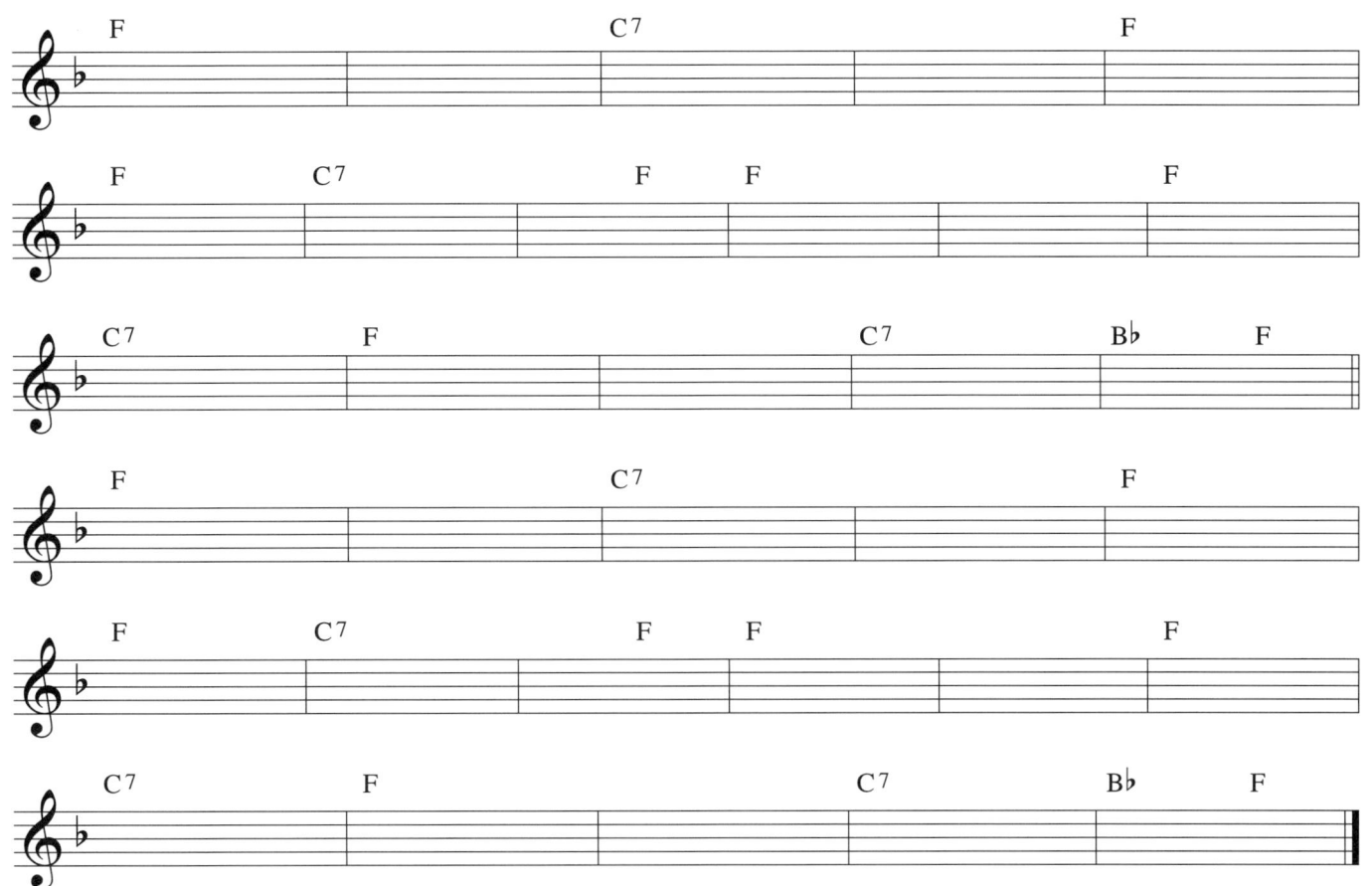

PART 1 – REPERTOIRE

When first learning "Down by the Riverside," cover the notation.

Down by
the Riverside
CD 2
Tracks 27–30

1. LISTEN to "Down by the Riverside" – melody (CD 2, Track 27) and bass line (CD 2, Track 28).

2. With the accompaniment (CD 2, Track 29) SING the melody by ear with words and on a syllable such as "doo" and SING the bass line by ear on "doo."

3. PLAY your instrument by ear on the clicks immediately following each melodic pattern (CD 2, Track 30).

4. With the accompaniment (CD 2, Track 29) PLAY the melody and bass line on your instrument with the appropriate style of articulation. Personalize the tune using expressive phrasing, dynamics, and tonal and rhythmic variation.

Down by the Riverside

American Folk Song

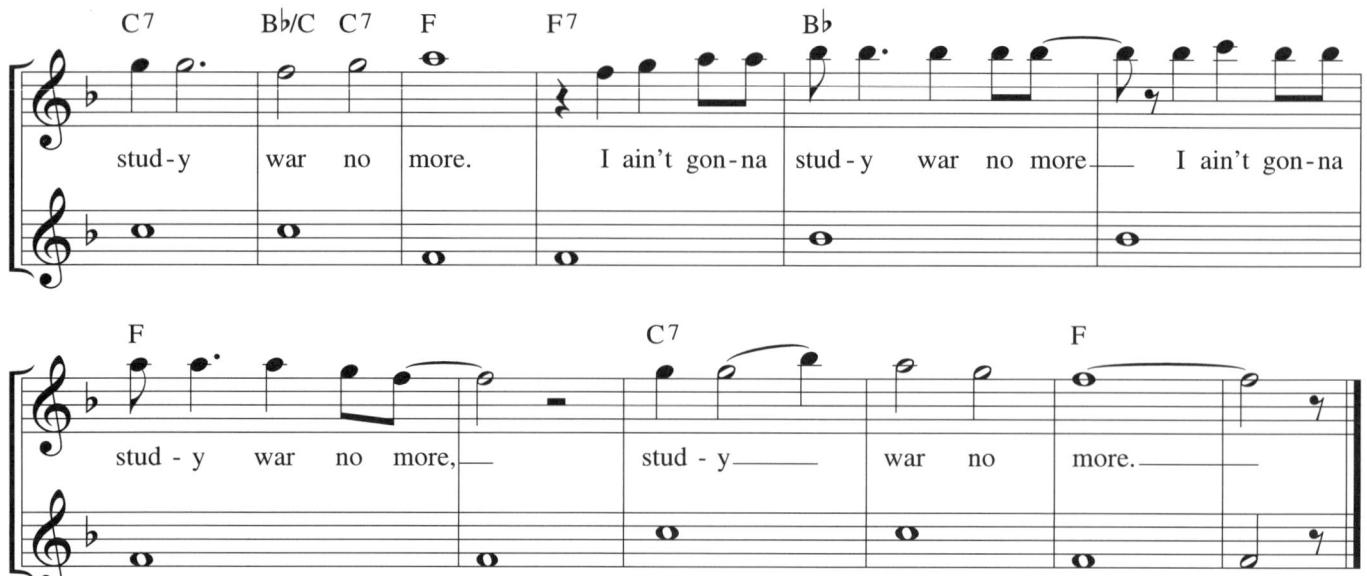

PART 2 – PATTERNS AND PROGRESSIONS

RHYTHM PATTERNS AND SERIES OF PATTERNS IN DUPLE METER (Swing Style)

Learn the patterns by ear – echo the patterns performed on the CD or by your teacher. When first learning the patterns, **cover the notation**.

Echo Rhythm Patterns for "Down by the Riverside"

Down by the Riverside CD 2 Tracks 31–32

Learning these patterns is similar to learning words in a language. Becoming familiar with these patterns will improve your vocabulary for improvising rhythms to this tune.

1. ECHO the duple patterns on the syllable "bah" – CD 2, Track 31.

2. ECHO the patterns with rhythm syllables – CD 2, Track 32. The rhythm syllables will help you to organize and remember the patterns.

3. ECHO the patterns on your instrument on F–DO. Use the style(s) of articulation appropriate for "Down by the Riverside." CD 2, Track 31 or 32.

The number (2) tells how many macrobeats (DU) are in a measure. The symbol (♩) indicates what kind of note is a macrobeat (DU). (♩=DU; ♩ ♩=DU DE; ♫♫ =DU DI DE DI)

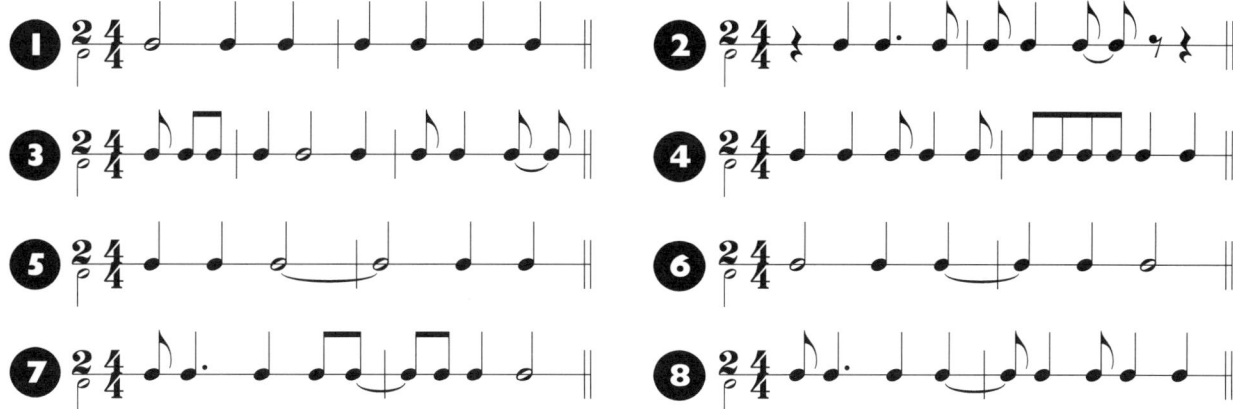

REPEAT AS NECESSARY

Improvise Rhythm Patterns for "Down by the Riverside"

Now that you are familiar with the rhythm patterns on CD 2, Tracks 31 and 32, improvise patterns using the rhythm vocabulary that you have learned.

Down by the Riverside CD 2 Tracks 31–32

1. Listen to the rhythm patterns performed on CD 2, Track 31. After each pattern, IMPROVISE a different pattern using the syllable "bah."

2. Listen to the rhythm patterns performed on CD 2, Track 32. After each pattern, IMPROVISE a different pattern using rhythm syllables.

3. IMPROVISE patterns on your instrument on F–DO. Use the style(s) of articulation appropriate for "Down by the Riverside." CD 2, Track 31 or 32.

Example:

LISTEN   IMPROVISE

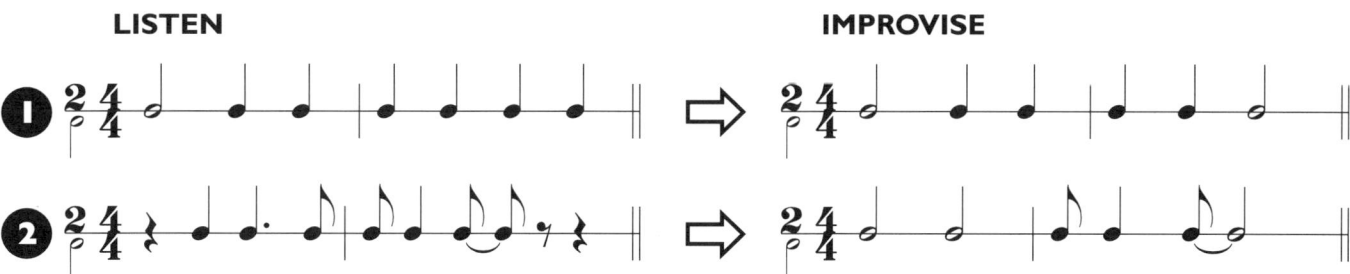

Continue with rhythm patterns 3 through 8 (CD 2, Tracks 31–32).

Echo and Improvise Series of Rhythm Patterns in Duple Meter

Down by the Riverside
CD 2
Tracks 33–34

Improvising a series of patterns is like speaking a sentence or phrase in language.

1. ECHO rhythm phrases using the syllable "bah" (CD 2, Track 33), with rhythm syllables (CD 2, Track 34), and with your instrument on F–DO (CD 2, Track 33 or 34).

2. After each rhythm phrase, IMPROVISE a different phrase using the syllable "bah" (CD 2, Track 33), with rhythm syllables (CD 2, Track 34), and with your instrument (CD 2, Track 33 or 34).

The number (2) tells how many macrobeats (DU) are in a measure. The symbol (♩) indicates what kind of note is a macrobeat (DU). (♩=DU; ♪ ♪=DU DE; ♫♫=DU DI DE DI)

TONAL PATTERNS AND HARMONIC PROGRESSIONS

You have just learned to improvise rhythm patterns and phrases of rhythm patterns. Now learn to improvise tonal patterns and harmonic progressions. Improve your tonal vocabulary by learning the following tonal patterns, first with a neutral syllable and then with solfège.

> Learn the patterns by ear – echo the patterns performed on the CD or by your teacher. When first learning the patterns, **cover the notation**.

Echo Tonal Patterns for "Down by the Riverside"

(F Major – Tonic, Subdominant, and Dominant)

1. SING the following patterns with the syllable "bum" (CD 2, Track 35).

2. Then, SING the following patterns with solfège (CD 2, Track 36).

3. PLAY each pattern on your instrument (CD 2, Track 35 or 36).

Establish Tonality (Concert Pitch)

Down by the Riverside
CD 2
Tracks 35–36

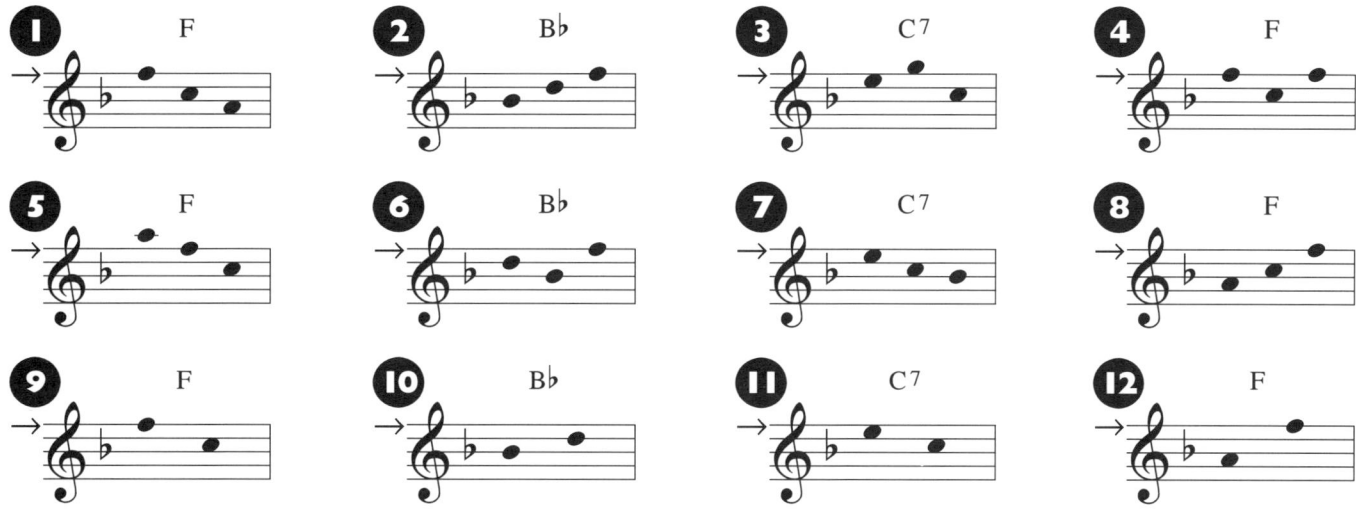

Repeat as Necessary

SING the Root (DO, FA, or SO) and NAME the Function (Tonic, Subdominant, or Dominant) in F Major

1. LISTEN to the tonal patterns performed on CD 2, Track 36. After each pattern, SING the root of that function using tonal syllables, and immediately identify the harmonic function. SING: "DO" and "Tonic," "FA" and "Subdominant," or "SO" and "Dominant." (F=Tonic; B♭=Subdominant; C7=Dominant)

2. LISTEN again, and PLAY the roots on your instrument.

Down by the Riverside
CD 2
Track 36

F indicates TONIC function, B♭ indicates a SUBDOMINANT function, and C7 indicates DOMINANT function. A TONIC pattern in major tonality includes any combination of "DO MI SO"; a SUBDOMINANT pattern includes any combination of "FA LA DO"; and a DOMINANT pattern includes any combination of "SO FA RE TI."

SOLFÈGE SHOULD ALWAYS BE SUNG–NOT SPOKEN

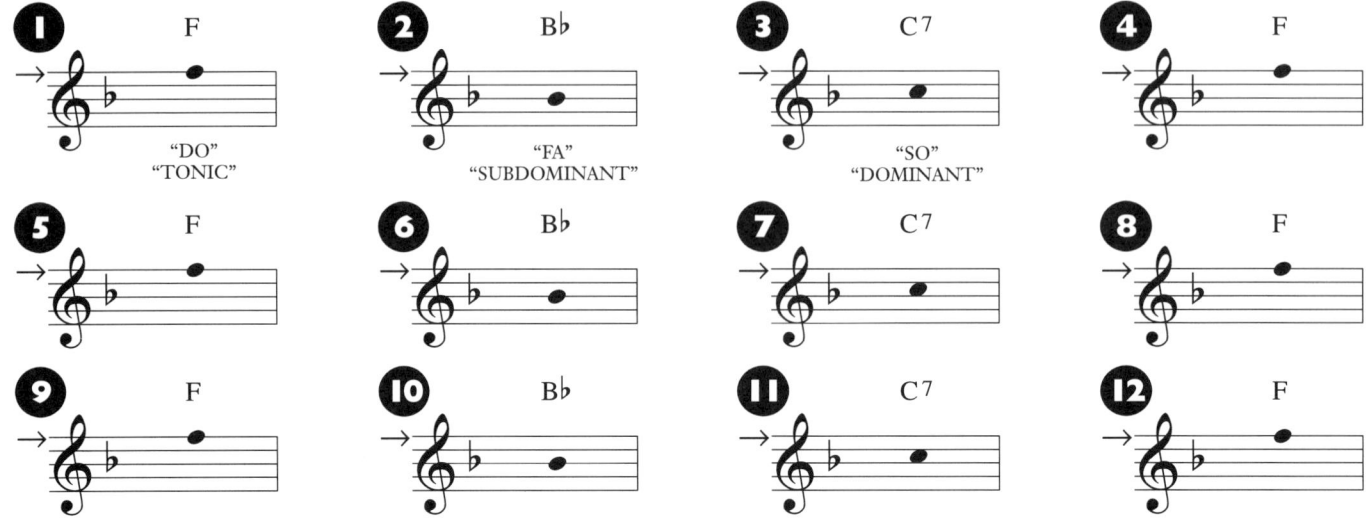

REPEAT AS NECESSARY

Improvise Tonal Patterns for "Down by the Riverside"
(Tonic, Subdominant, and Dominant Functions in F Major)

Down by
the Riverside
CD 2
Tracks 35–36

1. LISTEN again to the tonal patterns performed on CD 2, Tracks 35 and 36.

2. After each pattern, IMPROVISE a different pattern with the same harmonic function with a neutral syllable ("bum" – CD 2, Track 35).

3. After each pattern, IMPROVISE a different pattern with the same harmonic function with solfège (CD 2, Track 36).

4. After each pattern, IMPROVISE a different pattern with the same harmonic function on your instrument (CD 2, Track 35 or 36).

Example:

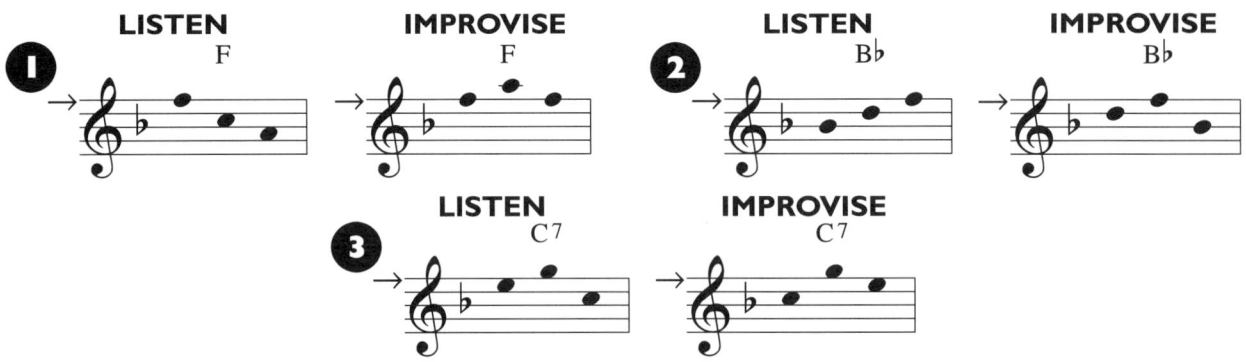

Continue with tonal patterns 4 through 12 (CD 2, Tracks 35–36).

ECHO and IMPROVISE Series of Tonic, Subdominant, and Dominant Patterns in F Major

Improvising a series of patterns to make a harmonic progression in music is like speaking a sentence or phrase in language. **Anticipate** and **predict** the harmonic progression. Where does the harmony go and where might it go?

1. Using the syllable "bum," ECHO (SING) the series of patterns (CD 2, Track 37).

2. Using solfège, ECHO (SING) the series of patterns (CD 2, Track 38).

3. ECHO the series of patterns on your instrument (CD 2, Track 37 or 38).

4. After each series of patterns, SING the bass line (roots) using solfège (CD 2, Track 38).

5. After each series of patterns, PLAY the bass line (roots) on your instrument (CD 2, Track 37 or 38).

6. After each series of patterns, IMPROVISE a different series of patterns over the same harmonic progression using solfège (CD 2, Track 38), with a neutral syllable ("bum" – CD 2, Track 37), and on your instrument (CD 2, Track 37 or 38).

Down by the Riverside
CD 2
Tracks 37–38

Example:

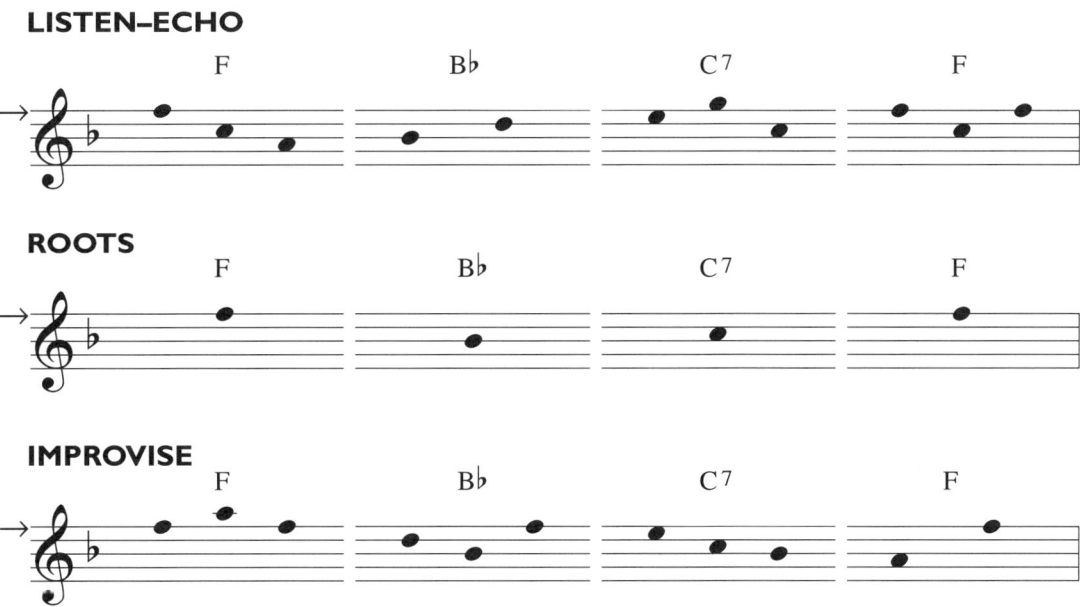

75

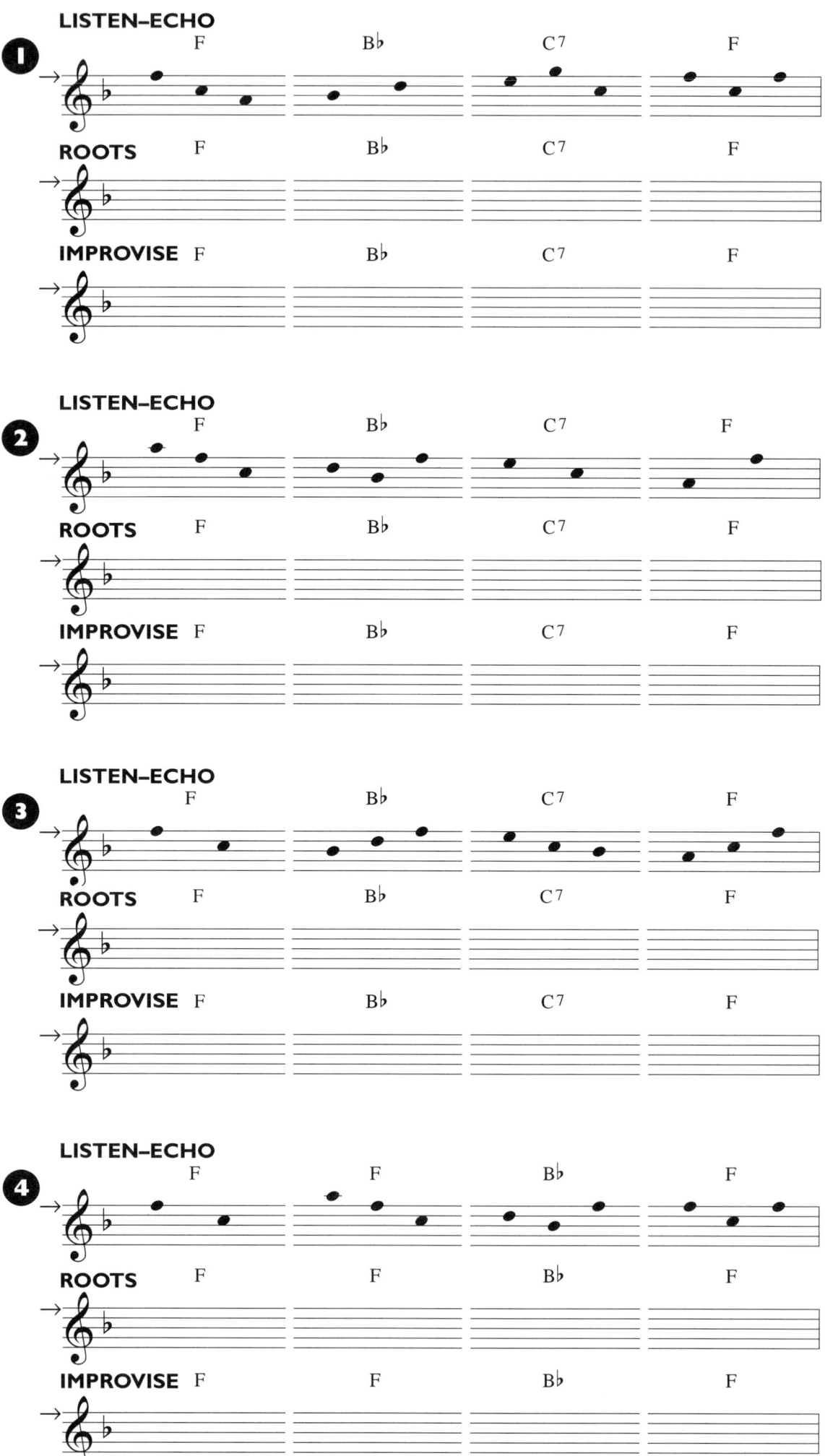

Sing improvised melodies to familiar repertoire.

1. Listen to CD 2, Track 39. The performer sings the first phrase (antecedent phrase) of "Down by the Riverside"; instead of continuing with the original second phrase (consequent phrase), you hear an improvised melody that continues the harmonic progression. Listen to all four antecedent phrases and improvised consequent phrases.

Down by the Riverside
CD 2
Track 39

Example:

Down by the Riverside

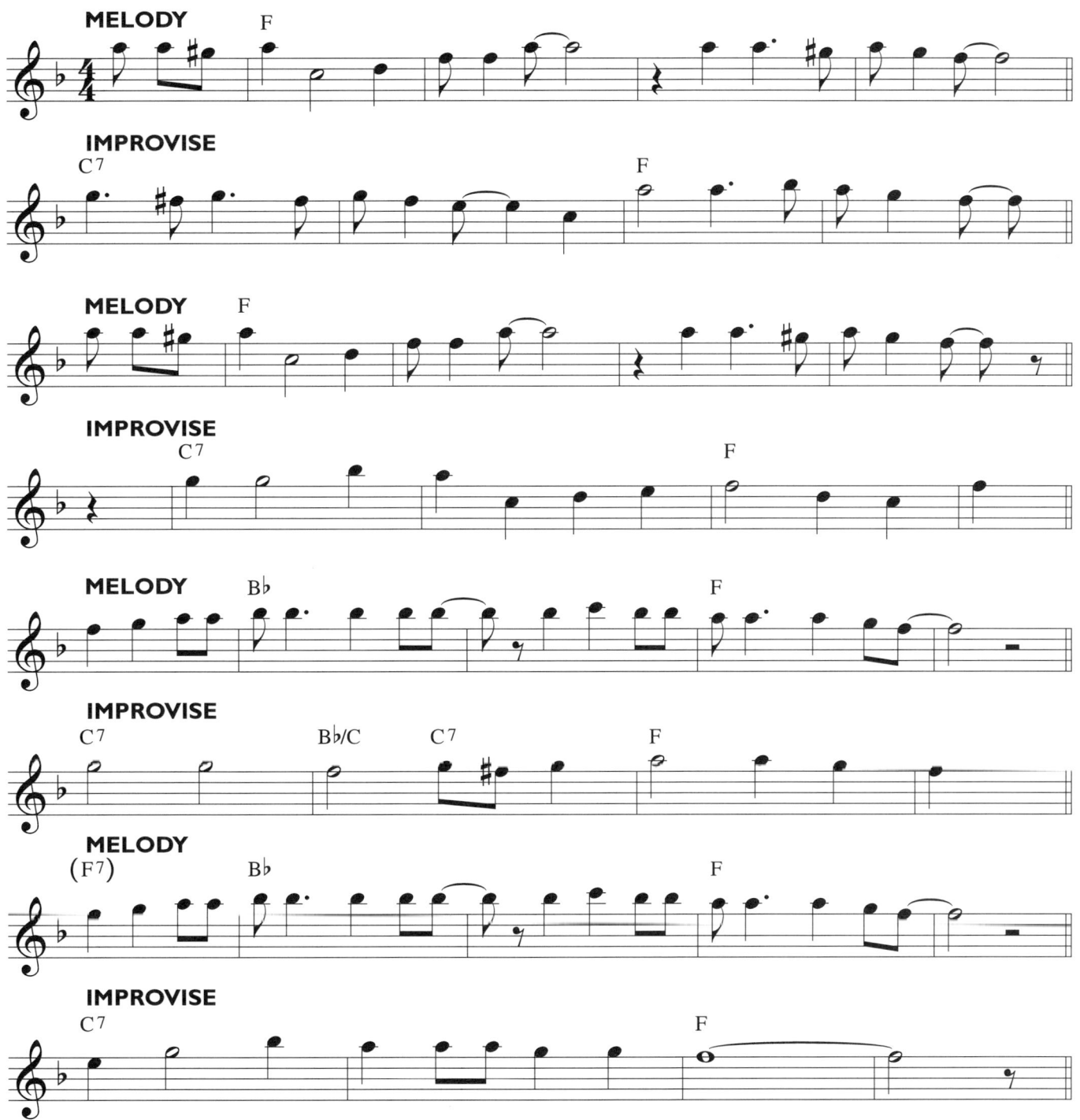

Down by the Riverside CD 2 Track 40

2. Listen to CD 2, Track 40. After hearing the first phrase (antecedent phrase) of "Down by the Riverside," continue the harmonic progression of the tune and sing a second phrase (consequent phrase) that is different from the original melody. Continue in a similar manner with the remaining phrases. Direct your melody toward chord tones, e.g., "DO," "MI," "SO" (CD 2, Track 40).

3. Perform in a similar manner on your instrument (CD 2, Track 40).

Now, you try:

Down by the Riverside CD 2 Track 49

4. Improvise both antecedent and consequent phrases to the harmonic progression of the tune (CD 2, Track 49). (The accompaniment repeats three times.)

SEVEN SKILLS

Before you begin the Seven Skills, review "Down by the Riverside" (CD 2, Tracks 27–30)

1. SING and PLAY the melody.

2. SING and PLAY the bass line (roots).

Skill I

1. Listen to CD 2, Track 41. The performer improvises rhythm patterns to the bass line of "Down by the Riverside."

> Down by
> the Riverside
> CD 2
> Tracks 27–30,
> 41

Example:

Down by the Riverside

2. Improvise rhythm patterns to the bass line of "Down by the Riverside." SING your improvisation with the neutral syllable "doo," and then PLAY it on your instrument (CD 2, Track 49).

Down by the Riverside CD 2 Track 49

Skill 2

1. Establish tonality in F major and SING each of the four parts below for the harmonic functions of "Down by the Riverside." For example, SING "DO, FA, SO, DO" – "DO, DO, TI, DO" – "MI, FA, FA, MI" – "SO, LA, SO, SO."

2. Play each part on your instrument.

When in a group setting, each student should select a part to sing and play for Skills 3 and 4. When performing alone, start with the bass line (chord roots – Skill 1) and then be sure to perform Skills 3 and 4 using the other three parts as well.

Example of Tonic, Subdominant, and Dominant Harmony in F Major – 4 Parts:

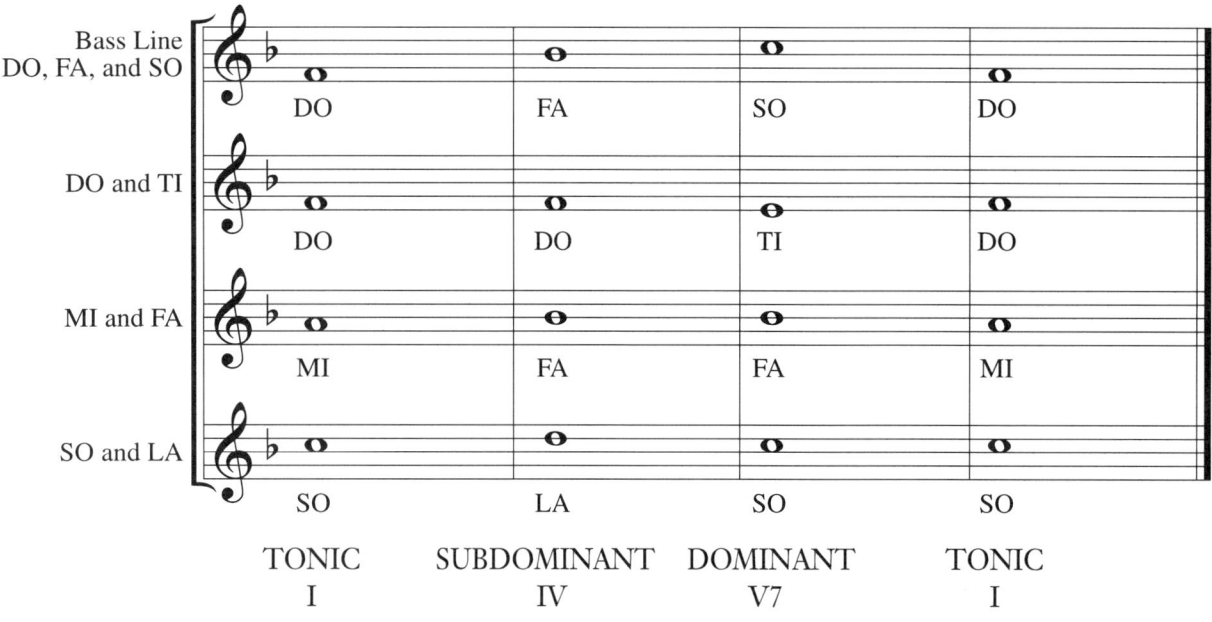

Skill 3

Down by the Riverside CD 2 Tracks 41, 49

Learn the harmonic rhythm for "Down by the Riverside" using the pitches from the harmony in **Skill 2**. SING every part. PLAY these parts on your instrument (CD 2, Track 49).

Skill 4

Using a neutral syllable (e.g., "doo"), improvise rhythm patterns to the harmonic progression using pitches learned in **Skill 2** (#2, 3, 4, and 5 starting on the facing page). Select a part and improvise rhythm patterns. Do this with each part. Interact with the melody (#1) and other parts (CD 2, Track 49). First SING, then PLAY these parts on your instrument. Listen to CD 2, Track 41 for an example using the bass line.

Down by the Riverside

MELODY

BASS LINE; IMPROVISE RHYTHM

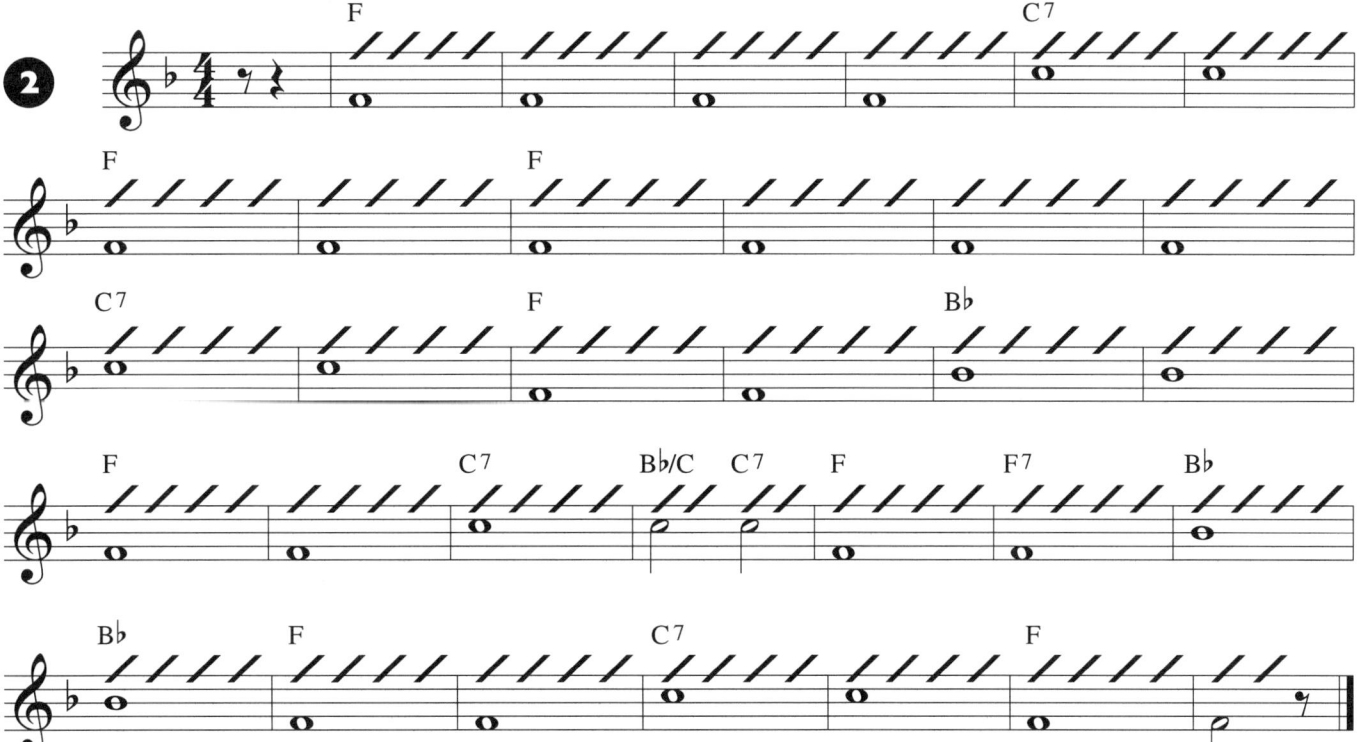

IMPROVISE RHYTHM ON "DO" AND "TI"

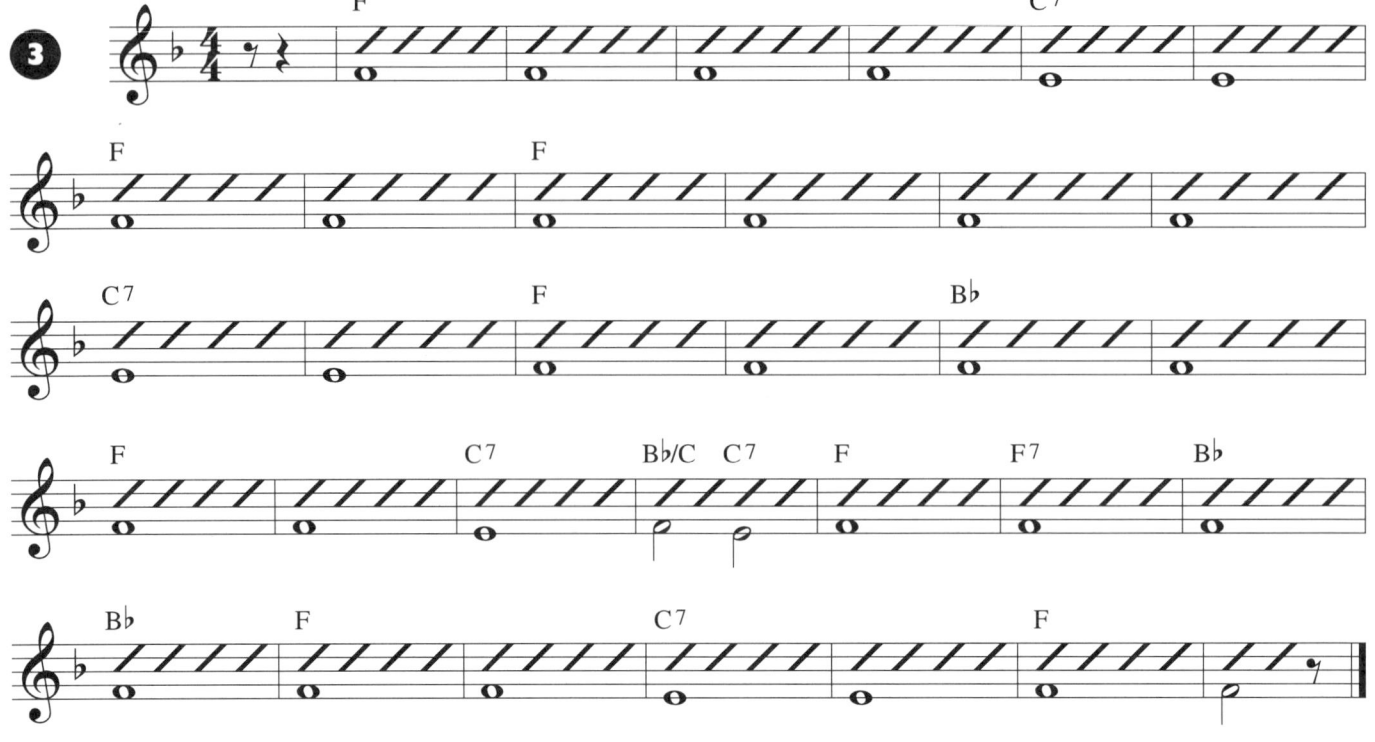

IMPROVISE RHYTHM ON "MI" AND "FA"

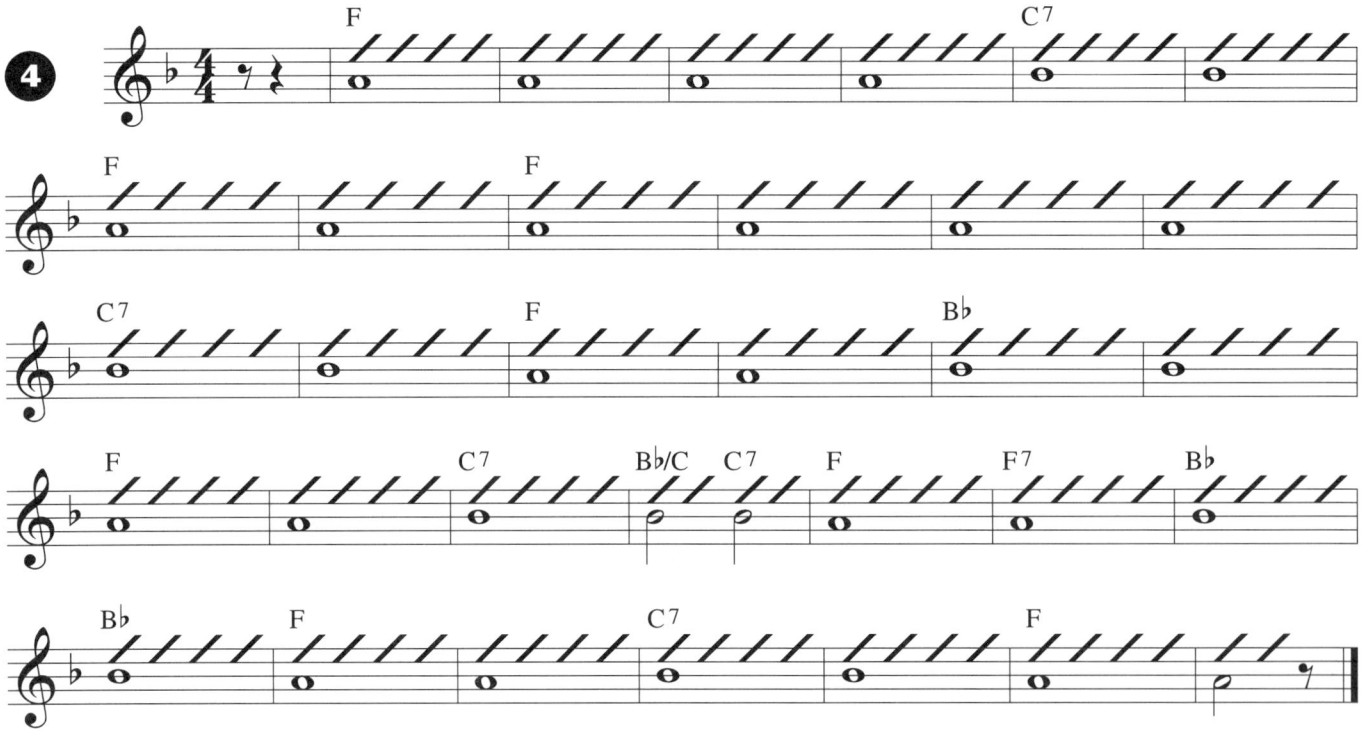

IMPROVISE RHYTHM ON "SO" AND "LA"

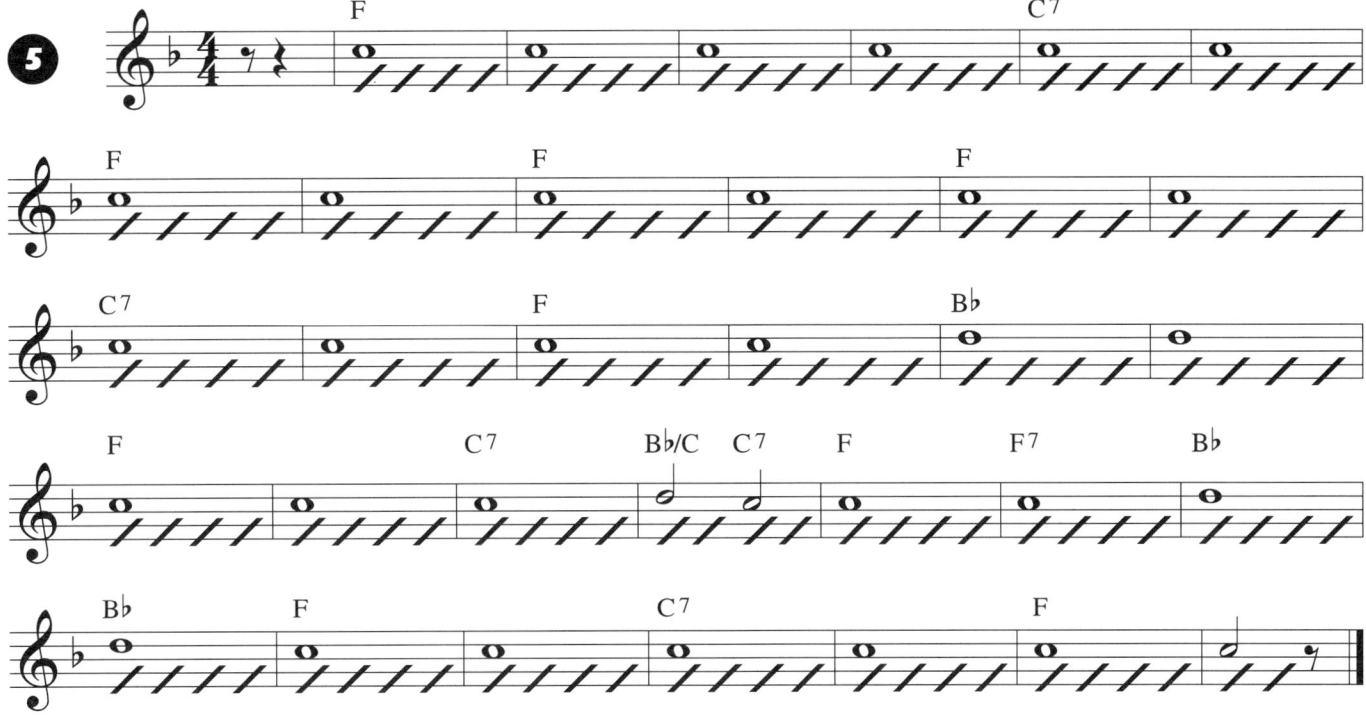

Skill 5

1. Listen to CD 2, Track 42. The performer improvises tonal patterns to the harmonic progression using macrobeats.

Down by the Riverside
CD 2
Track 42

Example:

2. Using macrobeats improvise (SING, then PLAY on your instrument) tonal patterns to the harmonic progression (CD 2, Track 49).

Skill 6

1. Listen to CD 2, Track 43. The performer improvises tonal patterns and rhythm patterns to the harmonic progression.

Example:

2. Improvise (SING, then PLAY on your instrument) tonal patterns and rhythm patterns to the harmonic progression (CD 2, Track 49).

Skill 7

1. Listen to CD 2, Track 44. The performer improvises by decorating and embellishing the melodic material in **Skill 6**.

Example:

2. Decorate and embellish the melodic material in **Skill 6**. Improvise melodies to the harmonic progression (CD 2, Track 49). Learn to SING and PLAY the solos provided (CD 2, Tracks 45, 46, 47, and 48).

Down by the Riverside CD 2 Tracks 45–49

IMPROVISE to "Down by the Riverside" (CD 2, Track 49). See page v for suggestions on developing meaningful improvisations.

PART 5 – READING AND WRITING

Rhythm Writing

1. Write the patterns on page 71 or notate improvised patterns. Establish meter and remember to group the notes into patterns and phrases before writing them.

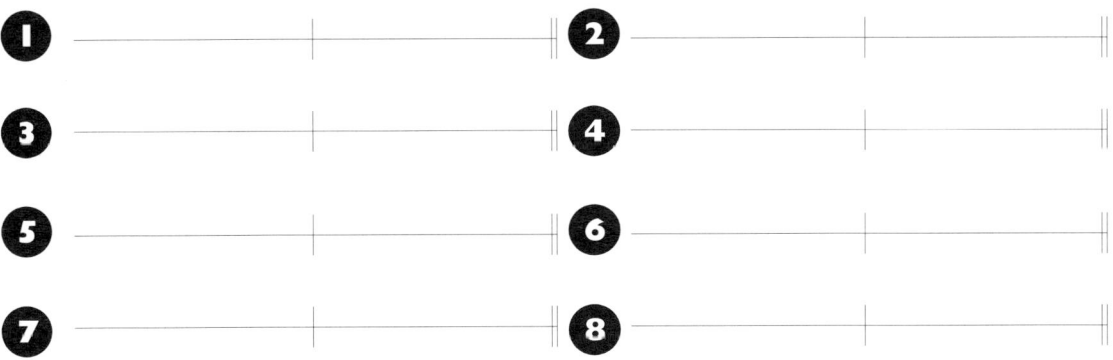

2. Write the series of patterns on page 72 or notate an improvised series of patterns.

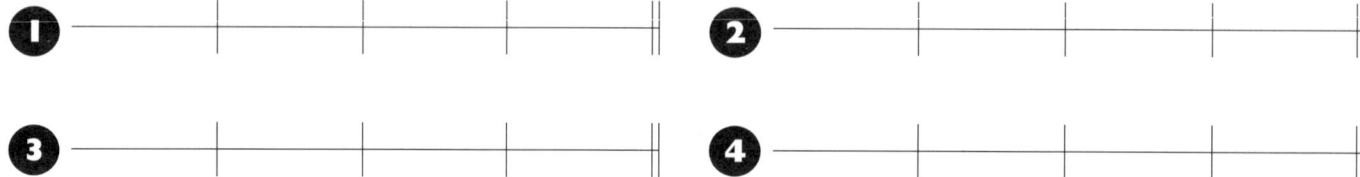

Tonal Writing

1. Write the patterns on page 73 or notate improvised patterns. Establish tonality and remember to group the notes into patterns and phrases before writing them.

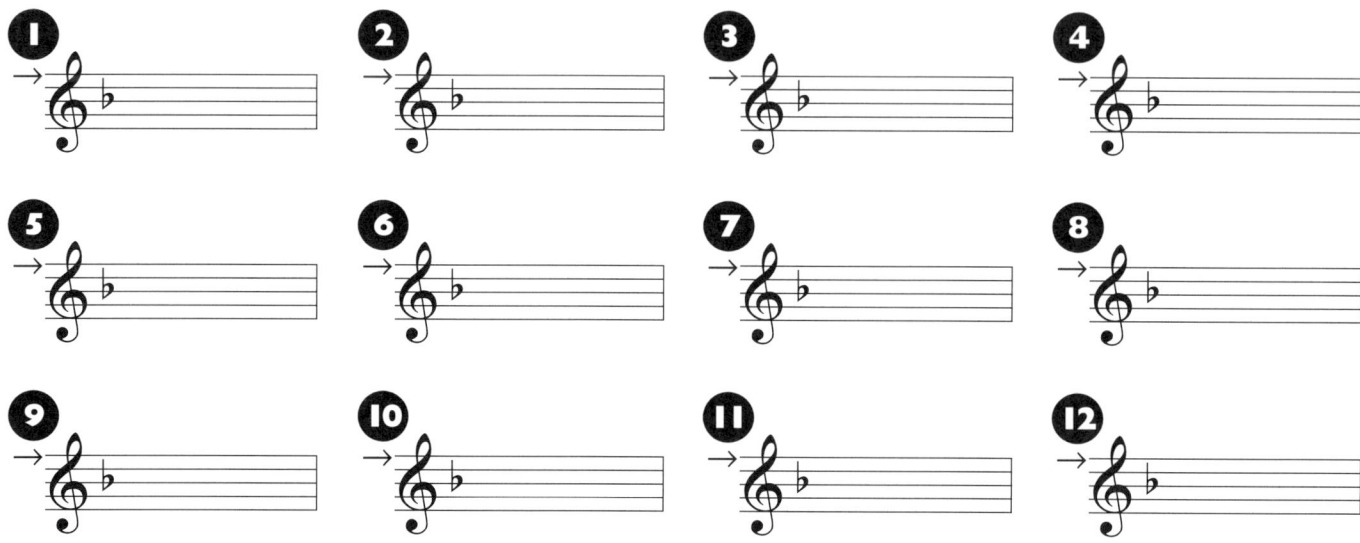

2. Write the series of patterns on page 76 or notate an improvised series of patterns for the progression.

READ "Down by the Riverside" and IMPROVISE to the harmonic progression (CD 2, Track 49). SING and PLAY the melody and/or bass line on your instrument. Also, COMPOSE other melodies using the harmonic progression indicated and the tonal and rhythm vocabulary that you have learned.

Down by the Riverside

MELODY

BASS LINE

IMPROVISE

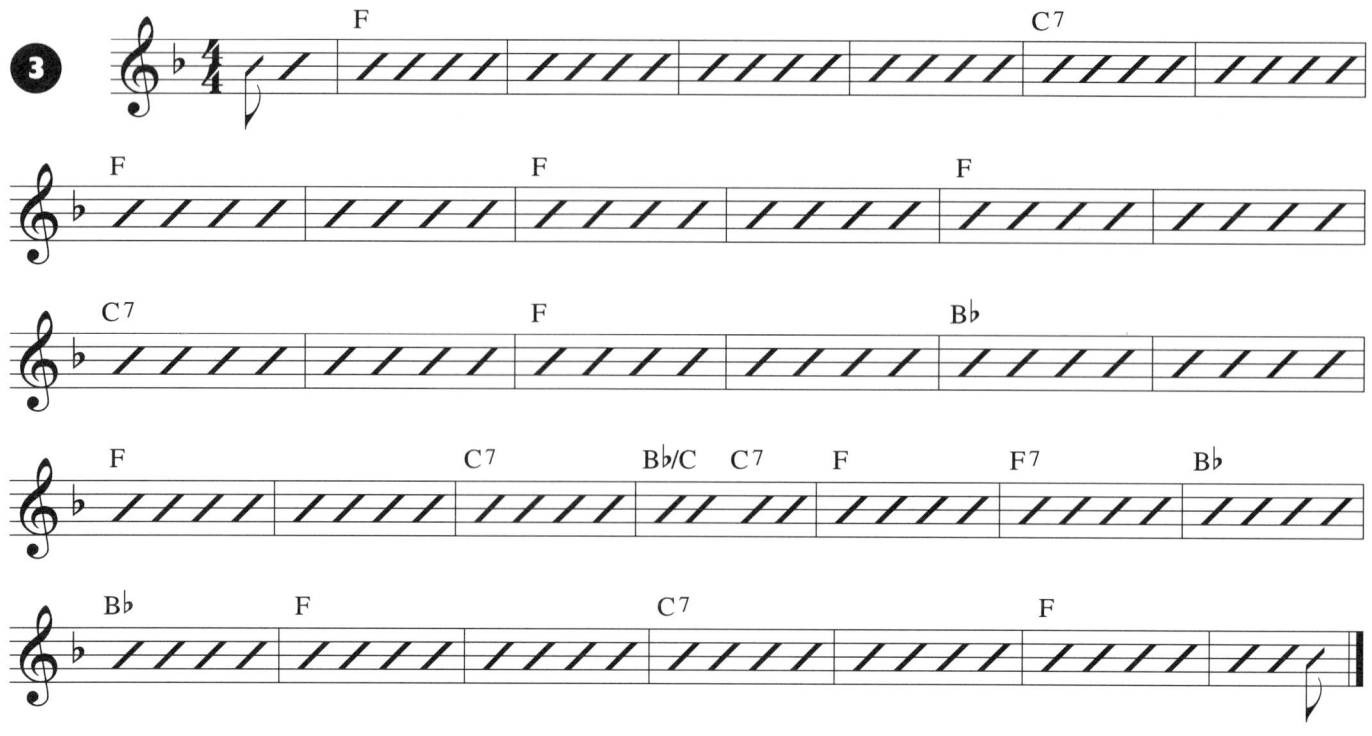

COMPOSE

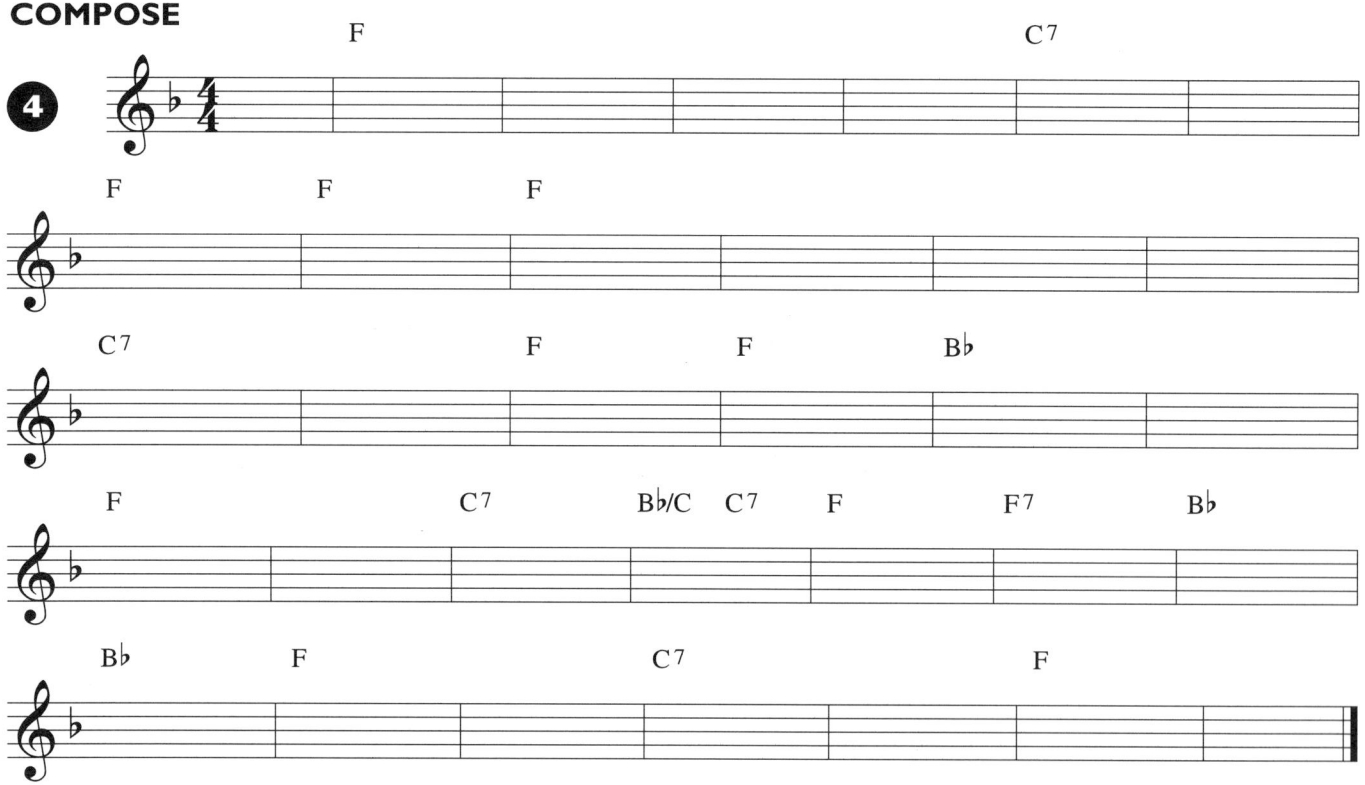

Listen to CD 2, Tracks 45–48. The performer plays an interpretation of the melody followed by an improvised solo. Learn to sing and play the solo performed on the CD. Use the space provided to finish transcribing the solo on CD 2, Track 45, or to notate other solos. Analyze the solos for vocabulary and ideas to incorporate into your own improvised solos. See page v for suggestions about developing meaningful improvisations. Perform with the accompaniment on CD 2, Track 49.

Down by the Riverside CD 2 Tracks 45–49

Down by the Riverside

The first 32 measures presented here were composed by Christopher Azzara – "Down by the Lakeside."